MISTAKE
POWER

MISTAKE POWER

The Investment Playbook for Women

How to Play the Game
In Good and Bad Times

JULIANA VILKE

Learn from the Mistakes of Others

"Never before has an investment guide
been so engaging, straightforward,
and easy to understand."

iUniverse LLC
Bloomington

Mistake Power
The Investment Playbook for Women

Copyright © 2013 by Juliana Vilke

All rights reserved. No part of this book may be used or reproduced by any means, graphic, electronic, or mechanical, including photocopying, recording, taping or by any information storage retrieval system without the written permission of the publisher except in the case of brief quotations embodied in critical articles and reviews.

iUniverse books may be ordered through booksellers or by contacting:

iUniverse LLC
1663 Liberty Drive
Bloomington, IN 47403
www.iuniverse.com
1-800-Authors (1-800-288-4677)

Because of the dynamic nature of the Internet, any web addresses or links contained in this book may have changed since publication and may no longer be valid. The views expressed in this work are solely those of the author and do not necessarily reflect the views of the publisher, and the publisher hereby disclaims any responsibility for them.

Any people depicted in stock imagery provided by Thinkstock are models, and such images are being used for illustrative purposes only.
Certain stock imagery © Thinkstock

ISBN: 978-1-4759-9811-5 (sc)
ISBN: 978-1-4759-9813-9 (hc)
ISBN: 978-1-4759-9812-2 (ebk)

Library of Congress Control Number: 2013912889

Printed in the United States of America

iUniverse rev. date: 09/14/2013

In Memory

Andy and Elsie M. Pedani,
Loving Parents

Contents

Acknowledgments xi
Preface xiii
Introduction xvii

1. **Surviving the Markets** 1
   A Backward Glance 2
   Creditable Market Indicators 6
   How Perception Affects Market Trends 7
   Takeaway 9

2. **Relying on Luck** 11
   Stock Market vs. the Economy 12
   Market Challenges 12
   Depressions and Recessions 14
   Identifying Recessions 15
   Past Recessions 16
   The Domino Effect 21
   Takeaway 24

3. **Risk vs. Reward** 27
   Emotions Rule 28
   Staying in the Game 33
   Kapitall, a Risk-Free Way to Learn from Mistakes ... 33
   Takeaway 34

4. **Game Changers** 35
   Shopping for a Financial Advisor 37
   Online Sites for Checking Out Financial Advisors ... 38
   Speculative Stocks 38
   Mutual Funds 39

    Reading the Prospectus 39
    Growth Mutual Funds 41
    Balanced Mutual Funds 44
    Bond or Income Mutual Funds.. 44
    Money Market Mutual Funds (MMFs)....................................... 44
    Check Out Mutual Funds before Investing 47
    Mutual Fund Jargon... 48
    Takeaway 49

5. **Confessions of the Rich and Famous**..**51**
    What You Can Learn from the Rich.. 53
    Fear of the Wall Street Cockroach 56
    Takeaway 57

6. **The Inside Scoop**..**59**
    The Art of Investing... 59
    Five Investment Strategies for Long-Term Investors 60
    Effects of Economic News.. 61
    Online Trading Pros and Cons 63
    Is Day-Trading Right for You?... 64
    Speculative Stock Picking... 67
    Day-Trading Stock Picks.. 68
    Chart Reading... 70
    Takeaway 71

7. **Cash Is King** **73**
    Takeaway 75

8. **Gold Magic**...**77**
    Gold-Producing Companies.. 78
    Gold Mutual Funds and Gold Commodity Funds 79
    The Rise and Fall of Gold 80
    Exchange-Traded Gold Funds 80
    Gold Krugerrand Coins 81
    Gold Jewelry 82
    Jewelers 82
    Takeaway 83

9. **Red Flags** **85**
   Takeaway 89

10. **Strategy Review** **91**
    Predictable and Preventable Mistakes 94

11. **Wall Street Lingo** **101**
    Banks with Economic Power 101
    Company Performance 102
    Contracts 102
    Dollar-Cost Averaging 103
    Indication of the Economy 103
    Investors 104
    Margin Buying or Leverage Buying 104
    Markets 104
    Orders 105
    Rates of Interest 106
    Securities Investor Protection Corporation (SIPC) 106
    Stocks 106
    Stock Market Indexes 107
    Trading Exchanges 108
    Values 109

Notes **111**

Index **119**

Acknowledgments

Mistake Power could not have been created by one person alone. I have had the good fortune to find some talented and caring individuals who have supported me in my endeavor.

I would especially like to thank my editorial consultant, George Nedeff, and my content editor, Terri Mauro, proof reader, Jo Ann Nelson, cover designer Reymond Mendez and everyone who contributed their advice and knowledge to making this book a valuable work that will benefit any woman who comes in contact with it.

On the home front, I'd like to thank my husband, John, for his help, patience, and understanding, and my sons, Gary, Stephen, and Kevin who are always willing to give a helping hand. Although my parents, Andy and Elsie Pedani, are no longer with us, I hope they will know I appreciate all they have done for me, and I want to say thank you, Mom and Dad.

We can learn a lot from the mistakes of other investors because most mistakes are caused by human nature. We all experience the same psychological biases and emotions. Therefore, we are all susceptible to making the same mistakes. Some of these mistakes can have a large impact on our wealth.[1]

—*John R. Nofsinger*

Preface

My fascination with the markets began as a youngster when my dad told stories about the madness of the Roaring Twenties. Conservative folks obsessed with magically becoming rich mortgaged their homes and plowed their savings into the risky stock market. When the inevitable happened, dreams were shattered, leaving many penniless and heartbroken. Amidst all the sorrow and suffering, some saw a buying opportunity. The risk takers purchased value stocks at rock-bottom prices and waited for the economy and the markets to improve. Eventually, the economy recovered, and the opportunists benefited.

Lessons in perception began in the 1940s as I traveled with my family by train from New York to our new home in Pennsylvania. A conductor came through the cabin loudly calling my name, and like any four-year-old fearing she may be in trouble, I slid down into my seat attempting to hide from this man. Although it appeared the conductor was looking for me, he was actually announcing the next train stop, Julian—an early demonstration that things are not always as they seem.

We arrived in Altoona amidst an explosion of autumn colors and found my dad's full-time job had been reduced to part-time status. In order to supplement his income, he purchased a truck and began delivering coal to folks needing it for heat. Although this business fit the profile for principles of profitability, it suffered due to customers being unable to pay for deliveries. While my mom struggled with finances, I learned about the perils of a small business and ultimately what is important in life. When the economy improved, my dad's work status returned to full-time, and I understood being rich had to do with what was in our hearts and not how much was in our bank accounts.

I later learned how a large bank account could be a tremendous enhancement to a virtuous heart.

Warren Buffett was only eleven years old when he made his first stock purchase of Cities Services Preferred, while I didn't make my first purchase of Penn Central until I was a teenager. After John and I got married, we chose to live simply and invest most of our disposable income in the markets. As our paper profits grew, our decision to live modestly turned out to be an excellent strategy.

> *I wish I could say our portfolio grew because I was an awesome investor. Actually, the stocks were held long-term to avoid paying high selling commissions.*

While accumulating a portfolio of best-of-breed stocks and diversifying into various mutual funds, commodity futures, and real property, John and I were blessed with three adorable children.

Seriously!

As our sons were growing up, we spent many of our days and evenings at the soccer, baseball, and football fields. My husband coached, and I often kept score. I did my share of carpooling, attending various school functions and field trips. Since my children were an integral part of my life, I juggled my various investment interests with their needs. I didn't begin day-trading until they were busy with their own careers. Kevin had passed the bar and was working long hours at a law firm. Stephen, a physicist working for NASA was writing computer programs in his time off, and Gary, an emergency-room doctor, was writing articles in his off hours. As you can see, my children didn't need me any longer, so I plunged into day-trading. The markets had always been my passion, and day-trading provided the adrenaline-charged stimulus I needed.

It was 1999, an exciting time in the market. Internet stocks were on a roll, and folks were reaping huge profits. Although most technology companies did not have earnings at that time, speculators plowed money into the market based on expectations of future earnings. After the NASDAQ peaked at 5,132.52 on March 10, 2000, the market began tumbling, picking up speed and bottoming out in 2001. Since dollar-cost averaging is generally a successful strategy when markets decline, I purchased additional shares of my favorite stocks at each market dip. Every morning when I turned on my computer, I found the market was down big, again and again. I wondered when was it going to stop, yet I continued to buy. In hindsight, the dips were not a market correction. It was the beginning of a devastating market crash.

While reviewing this mishap, I uncovered some compelling market information. This playbook is the composite of my research, plus lessons I learned over four decades of investing. It is my hope it will prove beneficial for women interested in increasing their net worth.

Mistake Power could not have been written without the love and support of my incredible husband, John Vilke, who never gave up on me. I hope this text will demonstrate I have learned from my mistakes, and although our children's inheritance is smaller, it is safer now.

> *This guide is a "twofer"—a useful tool for any woman willing to learn from the mistakes of others and an aide-mémoire for me.*

Those who fail to learn from history are doomed to repeat it.
—*Sir Winston Churchill*

Introduction

Based on four decades of investment experiences and extensive research, *Mistake Power* establishes how women can gain a competitive edge by identifying and eliminating investment mistakes. Advice is offered for those struggling with wealth-loss anxieties, yet the unfaltering objective is to offer women a reality check regarding the ramifications of repeating investment mistakes and following the crowd. Unlike a difficult and boring financial reference work, this text offers straightforward down-to-earth language, and an encouraging approach. The ethical implication of the research on these issues is reflected in the text.

Mistake Power summarizes and reflects on financial struggles in various situations from my perspective as a soccer mom and long-term investor turned obsessive day trader. Forthcoming regarding methods, supplements support experiences with research on the economy and its effect on markets. Timely, descriptive, and well-researched, *Mistake Power* includes a number of black-and-white photos of relevant entities. Women should find this text informative, enlightening, and engaging.

These are days when many are discouraged. In the ninety-three years of my life, depressions have come and gone. Prosperity has always returned and will again.
—John D. Rockefeller

1

Surviving the Markets

In the past, long-term investors who paid attention to daily market movements were usually better positioned when markets tanked. As the 2008 financial meltdown approached, some astute long-term investors sold their holdings and waited for the market to bottom before reinvesting into the 2009 lows. These investors are currently seeing profits soar, while others who didn't sell prior to the meltdown are only getting back to even.

Prior to 2007, the economy was thriving, so not many noticed the recession approaching. In a time of high home values, homeowners owned numerous piggyback and teaser-rate mortgages. *Mad Money's* Jim Cramer understood interest rates needed to be cut or homeowners would lose their homes and firms would go out of business. In August 2007, he publicly begged the Fed and Ben Bernanke to take action. Anyone who acted on his passionate plea most likely avoided the pitfalls of the financial meltdown. At that time, Bear Stearns stock traded at $109 a share; it fell to $2 by March 2008.[2] The company was later sold to JPMorgan Chase for $10 a share, or $240 million.

A Backward Glance

During the 1790s women in New York City were not interested in participating in financial endeavors, yet men met in various coffeehouses to gamble and barter. As time progressed, one of the coffeehouses near a large sycamore tree became a popular meeting site. Anyone not able to get inside the busy coffeehouse did business outside under the buttonwood, the popular name for the sycamore tree. During this time, twenty-four wealthy gentlemen familiar with many companies converted their knowledge and understanding into a business. They became middlemen—"brokers"—and charged a commission for their services. This exclusive boys' club became official on May 17, 1792, with the formal signing of the Buttonwood Agreement. Signed under the buttonwood tree, this simple promise to trade with each other and abide by a .25 percent commission was the beginning of the New York Stock and Exchange Board, now known as the NYSE or the New York Stock Exchange.[3]

As development continued over the years, the Wall Street wall—a wooden stockade built by the Dutch settlers to keep goats and hogs at bay—was removed. After the difficult days following World War I, the economy slowly improved and confidence returned. The second half of the twenties was an exciting time in America. The stock market was booming and ordinary folks could check the latest stock prices on ticker tape. Manufacturing establishments increased from 183,900 to 206,700, and automobile production grew from 4,301,000 to 5,358,000.[4] A fascination with wealth affected more people than ever before. As stock prices continued to climb, greed took hold, and folks gambled their savings in the risky stock market that was still dominated by men.

Decades later, in the early 1960s, many women still depended on their husbands for financial support. The good ol' boys club was tough to crack, but Muriel Siebert gained access in December 1967. She became the first woman to purchase a seat on the New York Stock Exchange, at a cost of $445,000. The seat was actually a symbolic depiction; instead of a tangible seat, she received a small oval white metallic badge with her name printed in black and the number 2646 printed in red. She claims it is the most expensive piece of jewelry she owns.[5]

While Muriel Siebert was getting used to wearing her expensive new jewelry at the NYSE, women were focusing on saving and having enough insurance to protect them and their children in case of an unforeseeable event. Following this adjustment, women began looking at alternative investments as a means to increase their financial net worth.[6] As women gained confidence, they got on the fast track, getting college degrees and entering the business world. By 2006, women twenty-five and older held nearly as many college degrees as men, 26.8 million for women versus 26.9 million for men. Out of roughly 10.4 million US privately owned firms, at least half were owned by women.[7] Although women have made many advances in business, there remains a misconception that they are ignorant about investing details and prefer to leave financial planning to others.

Powerful Women in 2007[8]

Woman	Title	Company	Country
Angela Merkel	Chancellor		Germany
Ho Ching	Chief Executive	Temasek Holdings	Singapore
Indra Nooyi	Chief Executive	PepsiCo	USA
Patricia Woertz	Chief Executive	Archer Daniels Midland	USA
Irene Rosenfield	Chief Executive	Kraft Foods	USA
Patricia Russo	Chief Executive	Alcatel-Lucent	USA
Anne Mulcahy	Chief Executive	Xerox	USA

Angela Braly	Chief Executive	Well Point	USA
Brenda Barnes	Chief Executive	Sara Lee Corp.	USA
Ruth Bader Ginsburg	Supreme Court Justice		USA
Oprah Winfrey	Chairman	Harpo	USA
Margaret Whitman	Chief Executive	EBAY	USA
Hillary Clinton	Senator		USA
Nancy Pelosi	Speaker/House of Representatives		USA
Safra Catz	President	Oracle	USA
Susan Arnold	President, Global Business Units	Procter & Gamble	USA
Drew Faust	President	Harvard University	USA

Wealthy Self-Made Women in 2011[9]

Oprah Winfrey: successful TV talk host launched OWN cable station (USA)
Jin Sook Chang: chief merchandising officer of Forever 21 chain (USA)
Meg Whitman: former eBay chief, joined VC firm Kleiner Perkins (USA)
Wu Yajun: runs Beijing developer Longfor Properties (China)
J.K. Rowling: author of Harry Potter series (UK)

Only a limited number of successful women are listed above, yet these lists show how far women have come. Several contemporary women not listed above who stand out for their roles in the advancement of women are Muriel Siebert, Suze Orman, and Martha Stewart. Muriel—as previously mentioned, the first woman to own a seat on the NYSE—has been encouraging women to take control of their own financial futures since the sixties. Suze, another advocate for taking control of finances, offers a wealth of information during her speaking engagements and in her many books. Martha, a successful business guru, is proof a woman can overcome any obstacle. Another woman listed above who deserves a special expression of gratitude for her significant contribution to the advancement of women is Oprah Winfrey, a child-prodigy orator who began her career at the age of three and a half when she gave James Weldon Johnson's sermons in various churches in Nashville.[10]

Empowered in businesses, women have taken their comfort to a new level. The following photos show some changes modern women have adopted.

Modern women have opted to wear comfortable, less-constricting garments.

Bathing suits have gotten smaller and more comfortable over the years.

Creditable Market Indicators

Many changes have occurred over the years, yet history can provide an indication of what we may expect in the future. When circumstances are similar, certain actions are predictable and thus preventable. Prior to both the 1929 market crash and the 2001 tech debacle, investors had a false sense of security in the markets. Thinking prices would continue moving up forever, they plowed money into the market highs.

In hindsight, we know these upside movements could not be sustained, and both markets fell precipitously. On September 3, 1929, the Dow peaked at 381 before beginning to decline, accelerating on the way down until the market crashed seven weeks later. This action is similar to the technology spike on March 10, 2000, followed by the burst of the tech bubble in 2001.

In the first five months of 2013, the Dow has been making new daily highs, closing at 15,105.12 on May 8, 2013. Investors are trying to determine whether to continue buying or whether it is time to sell into the highs. When attempting to make an informed decision, pay attention to volume and the number of investors who are still out of the game. As a general rule, markets don't change direction until there is full saturation, so it may be in your best interest to stay in the game. Of course, rules are meant to be broken, so take precautions like issuing a stop-loss order to keep from losing more than a predetermined amount of money in case of a premature reversal.

How Perception Affects Market Trends

One culprit in changing the complexion of the market is perception. Investors sometimes find themselves convinced that a problem has been eradicated when in fact it still exists. Prior to the 2007 recession, the economy and the housing market were thriving, so it was difficult to spot a recession on the horizon. Since not many noticed as the recession approached, countless folks continued to make purchases and hold financials they should have sold. Anyone who gave credence to Jim Cramer's plea to the Fed most likely sold and avoided the downfall. As financials fell, many investors took it as a buying opportunity or a market correction when in fact it was a financial market crash.

During the 2001 dot-com crash, perception of the market plunge was also a misjudgment. Even though the pullback was larger than normal, many investors perceived the plunge as a market correction. They continued to hold stocks they should have sold or purchase additional shares of stocks they already owned in an attempt at dollar-cost averaging.

The 1929 market crashed in the morning, yet it closed up at day's end after Thomas W. Lamont held a press conference successfully convincing investors that better days were ahead. The same problems existed, but because Lamont was successful in changing investor perception, many folks continued to hold stocks they should have sold. The following synopsis of the days following the 1929 market crash can provide valuable insight if similar circumstances are encountered in the future.[11]

1929 Market Crash

Day 1: October 24, 1929—Black Thursday
- Stock prices suddenly plunged in the morning.
- Bankers who later became known as the White Knights held a lunchtime meeting to try to avert the market problem.
- Thomas W. Lamont, a partner at J.P. Morgan and one of the White Knights, held a press conference after the meeting and was successful in presenting a hopeful outlook for the future.
- The market actually closed up this day as well as the next day. In hindsight, we know this was a skewed perception.

Day 2: October 25, 1929
- The markets closed up again as investors perceived the problems to be over.
- In hindsight, we know the problems still existed and the perception was incorrect.

Day 5: October 28, 1929—Bloody Monday
- The markets opened with aggressive selling.
- Perception changed and markets plunged all day.

Day 6: October 29, 1929—Black Tuesday
- Markets were in free fall again.
- A record volume of stocks were traded this day.

Day 7: October 30, 1929
- It was perceived the worst was over, as speculators returned to the markets.
- In hindsight, we know this was a delusion.

Day 13: November 13, 1929
- It appeared markets had bottomed.
- The real bottom occurred two and a half years later.

July 8, 1932
- The Dow Jones bottomed.
- Great Depression did not hit bottom until nearly a year later.

March 1933
- Great Depression hit bottom, three and a half years after the 1929 market crash.

November 1954
- Markets got back to even twenty-five years after the market crash.
- Republican President Dwight D. Eisenhower was in office from 1953 1961.

Karen Blumenthal, *Six Days in October: The Stock Market Crash of 1929*.

During market recovery, value investors begin nibbling at best-of-breed stocks, while others sit on the sidelines unwilling to risk additional losses. After the 1929 market plunges, speculators profited by buying at market lows and selling after the market made ample gains.

- John D. Rockefeller and his son began purchasing stocks of excellent companies.
- Henry Ford cut car prices by $15. The price of the Ford Coup dropped to $35.
- Legend has it Albert H. Wiggin, chairman of Chase National Bank, promoted the recovery process by suggesting it was a buying opportunity. While his bank was purchasing best-of-breed stocks, he was shorting them. Wiggins made a personal profit of several million dollars from his short trades, and his earnings were tax-free because he used a Canadian company to buy the stocks.[12]
- Legend has it that anyone investing $10,000 in General Motors in the early twenties and selling prior to the 1929 market crash would have made a tidy profit of over $1.5 million. However, those who held the stock until after the crash would have seen the profit wiped out. During the days following the crash, many stocks were worth a small fraction of what they were worth a year earlier. US Steel fell from $205 to $21.25 per share, and Radio fell from $110 to $2.50. This compares to the 2001 tech debacle, when JNPR fell from $200 a share to $11 and JDSU fell from $150 to $14. These stock prices also compare to the behavior of stocks like Citicorp during the 2007 to 2009 recession, falling from $52 a share to $3.[13]

> *Buying value stocks at rock-bottom prices and selling into highs is an excellent strategy.*

Takeaway

- During the 1790s, women in New York City were not interested in financial endeavors, yet men met in various coffeehouses to gamble and barter. The New York Stock and Exchange board became official on May 17, 1792, and is now known as the NYSE.

- Women did not become interested in the financial world until decades later, during the 1960s, when Muriel Siebert purchased a seat on the NYSE.
- As women gained confidence, they got on the fast track, getting college degrees and becoming successful in the business world.
- By 2006, women twenty-five and older held nearly as many college degrees as men—26.8 million for women versus 26.9 million for men. Out of roughly 10.4 million US privately owned firms, at least half were owned by women.
- Many changes have taken place over the years, but history remains a good indication of the future.
- Investors who pay attention to creditable market indicators are better positioned when markets tank.
- Investors who purchase stock at the market peaks usually suffer large losses.
- Perception can change the complexion of the market, often causing many to lose their fortunes.
- During the recovery process from a recession or depression, speculators usually begin nibbling at best-of-breed stocks. After value investors make purchases at market lows, they generally hold the stocks long-term.
- During the 1929 market crash, the Dow plunged in the morning yet closed up at day's end because perception of the market was changed by a banker indicating better days were ahead. In hindsight, we know the same problems still existed, and the market plummeted several days later.
- During the 2001 tech debacle, traders and fund managers who treated the declines as a normal pullback instead of a market crash suffered huge losses.
- At the onset of the 2007 recession, it was difficult to believe a recession was on the horizon, since the economy and the housing market were flourishing. Recessions usually follow times of exuberance.

Although women have made many advances in business, there remains a misconception that women are ignorant about investing details and prefer to leave financial planning to others. **Women working together can make this misunderstanding vanish.**

I don't know where the stock market is going, but I will say this, that if it continues higher, this will do more to stimulate the economy than anything we've been talking about today.[14]

—*Alan Greenspan*

2

Relying on Luck

A Fool's Game

Where is the economy headed? This question has plagued investors for decades and is particularity troublesome as economic cycles evolve. Contrary to popular belief, markets trending up can be as problematic as markets trending down in a slowing economy if the investor is sitting on the sidelines waiting for another downturn that may not occur. This emotional experience can be nearly as strong as owning stocks when markets tank (see chapter 3). Behavior analysts studying investor reactions found that both men and women react to market stimuli in a similar manner, and because men have been investing in markets longer than women, many findings presented in this text are compared to strategies implemented by successful men.

Stock Market vs. the Economy

The stock market is thought to be six months ahead of where the economy is headed. In an attempt to extrapolate the truth from various posturing, it is often difficult to see where we are headed unless we look at where we've been. Of course, the future is never certain, but when we take a backward glance, the pathway may begin to make sense. We should tread lightly and pay careful attention to various economic indicators, such as interest rates, down-payment requirements, production changes, housing shifts, consumer demands, unemployment reports, and market trends. Noting subtle changes occurring in our lives and in the lives of our family, friends, and neighbors can help substantiate our findings. Checking out retail establishments and discount malls can be both informative and fun. If all else fails, some say we should rely on luck.

Luck, really?

Legend has it that Joseph Kennedy relied on luck when he sold all his stock the day before the 1929 stock market crash. According to the story, back in the twenties, only the rich and powerful purchased stock; when Kennedy got a stock tip from a shoeshine boy, he became suspicious, thinking a shoeshine boy should not be so knowledgeable about the markets. From this encounter, Kennedy determined the market must be oversaturated, and he decided to sell. Since his timing was excellent, many refer to this action as being lucky.[15]

Was Kennedy lucky, or did his gut instinct prove accurate based on his keen sense of observation?

Market Challenges

Investors worry as the economy slows, yet they are less concerned when inflation is on the horizon. Depending on how administrations handle problems, economies can either move forward or retreat. During the evolution process, deflation, inflation, or stagflation can creep up without being noticed. As the economy was booming throughout the second half of the 1920s, optimism reigned supreme. Late-to-the-party folks borrowed money to purchase stocks as though the markets would move higher forever. When the weeks leading to the 1929 market crash showed subtle signs the market was slowing, not many noticed. A few astute investors suspected trouble because of fewer homes being built, failing banks, and a decline in steel production. Guided by these observations, they strayed from the masses and sold into the highs. In hindsight, we know these investors profited while others sustained huge losses.

Deflation may be ignored as it approaches because of the good times preceding it. Deflation comes on slowly but can accelerate quickly as banks and lending institutions tighten their purse strings. When consumers are unable to access credit, work orders are cancelled. Businesses relying on those orders attempt to remain solvent by implementing massive layoffs. In spite of cost-saving devices, many of these businesses fail, leaving more unemployed. As the domino effect continues, nearly everyone is affected in some way. Laid-off employees cannot keep up with credit obligations. Property owners default, causing home prices to decline. Loans are unobtainable, keeping buyers out of the marketplace. There are many bargains, but cash is often unobtainable. The bears stay in command, and trepidation about the future becomes the norm.

Inflation may also approach without much notice because of the difficult times preceding it. Prices begin to rise slowly in necessary services like utilities, commodities, and housing. Rents go up. Purchasing power is significantly reduced as incomes do not keep up with skyrocketing prices. During these times, some companies emerge as winners. The job openings in these winning sectors often exceed the number of applicants, causing employers to offer incentives in order to attract and keep qualified personnel. With the excessive number of jobs lost in the 2007 recession, it is difficult to envision that numerous job openings could ever be problematic, but for firms understaffed at the onset of high inflation, it's a definite problem. Some firms cope by offering full-time employees additional compensation to work overtime, while others hire temporary placement specialists. These problem-solving techniques have the unintended consequences of inefficiency and smaller profits.

Stagflation is difficult to recognize because it occurs when commodity prices and inflation are high while economic growth is low thanks to high unemployment. Stagflation is often ignored even though commodity prices, utilities, and services continue to rise. Consumers and businesses tighten their belts. During the stagflation of the seventies, economic growth slowed, interest rates remained high, and property values fell as home-buying came to a standstill. In 2011, the economic situation in the United States nearly resembled stagflation: unemployment was high while economic growth and home-buying were low. By keeping interest rates low, the Obama administration, Ben Bernanke, and the Federal Reserve were successful in averting stagflation. Only the future will determine if the good times continue.

> *Particularly troublesome are markets evolving from inflationary times, since they are often a precursor to a recession.*

Depressions and Recessions

The following historical data, including investor reactions, may prove valuable for anyone sitting on the fence during similar economic conditions. Market survival is usually challenging as economic cycles evolve. Market technicians believe history repeats itself as the economy oscillates between good and bad times. It is their belief that the outcome of past experiences can be a creditable indicator of what may or may not work in the future.

A depression is often defined as a recession that lasts longer than three or four years or a severe downturn—10 percent or more—of the gross domestic product. Historically, America has had many recessions but only one depression. The recession that began in December 2007 often looked similar to a depression, but thanks to the outstanding response of the Fed and Ben Bernanke, a depression was avoided.

Interestingly, many historians refuse to accept that America was ever in a depression. Those who accept it was a depression often disagree about the cause. Some believe the stock market crash was the cause, while others disagree and argue the crash was only the symptom and not the problem. These historians insist there were many other issues leading to the crash, such as bank failures, unemployment, and loss of business profits. After their wealth was slashed, the rich scaled back from making many of the luxury purchases that keep the economy going.[16] This inaction by the rich caused the economy to remain slow. In hindsight, increasing taxes on the rich is never a good idea when the economy is fragile.

The Great Depression followed the 1929 market crash. In addition to economic problems resulting from the crash, the Great Plains area was hit with dust storms caused by high winds. As loose dirt whirled about, crops were damaged and anything in the storm's path was destroyed. Many small farmers had debt problems that multiplied after the dust storms. When they were unable to make payments on loans, banks foreclosed, leaving farmers and their families homeless and unemployed.[17] The Great Depression bottomed three and a half years after the 1929 market crash. It took twenty-five years for the market to get back to even. In comparison, the Dow high of 13,892.54 on October 17, 2007, was followed by a March 2009 low of 7,170.06. The Dow nearly got back to even on October 22, 2012, closing at 13,343.51. As of April 2013, the Dow has been closing over 14,500, heading toward 15,000.[18]

A recession is defined as a downturn in the gross domestic product for six months or at least two successive quarters or more.[19] During recessions, the job market appears to dry up, but specific skill-type jobs, as well as low-paying jobs, are often left unfilled.

Historically, many of our ancestors took low-paying jobs because they were willing to work several jobs. Having arrived in America from communist and socialistic countries, they were willing to work three jobs if necessary in order to keep their newfound freedoms and preserve their independence. Their past experiences taught them the ramifications of a "free lunch." Given handouts by their governments, they became unproductive, needy, and controllable. With no formal education and limited command of the language, my grandma escaped this life. Although she found herself in an underdeveloped area of America, she felt fortunate to have her freedom.

Identifying Recessions

There have been many variations of recessions in the United States. Some have been long in duration, while others have been short. To help identify the different types of recessions, many are given alphabetical names. The four general types are V-shaped, W-shaped, L-shaped, or U-shaped. The letter symbolizes the course of the recession. For example, the left side of the V displays the decline and the upturn indicates quick improvement, while the W shows there was a double dip: V + V = W. The L is a sharp decline extending sideways, indicating that the economy does not improve rapidly, whereas the U declines and remains at the bottom longer than a V before improving.

Name	Economy	Type	Years
V-shaped recession	Rising inflation, high interest rates, and high unemployment	Short/sharp	1954 1990–1991
U-shaped stagflation recession	High inflation, high interest rates, and high unemployment	Prolonged slump	1973–1975
W-shaped recession	High inflation, high interest rates, and high unemployment	Double dip	1/1980–7/1980 7/1981–11/1982
L-shaped recession	Rising inflation, low interest rates, and high unemployment	Sharp downturn	2007–2009

Past Recessions

Reviewing actions taken by various administrations to avert problems during past recessions provides insight into how similar actions may affect future economies.

February 1945 to October 1945
- *Type:* recession
- *Duration:* eight months
- *Administrations:* Franklin D. Roosevelt (through April 1945) and Harry S. Truman

November 1948 to October 1949
- *Type:* recession
- *Duration:* eleven months
- *Administration:* Harry S. Truman

July 1953 to May 1954
- *Type:* L-shaped recession
- *Duration:* ten months
- *Administration:* Dwight D. Eisenhower

August 1957 to April 1958
- *Type:* recession
- *Duration:* eight months
- *Administration:* Dwight D. Eisenhower

April 1960 to February 1961
- *Type:* recession
- *Duration:* ten months
- *Administration:* Dwight D. Eisenhower (ended in January 1961)

December 1969 to November 1970
- *Type:* mild recession
- *Duration:* eleven months
- *Administration:* Richard Nixon

The eleven-month recession that started in December 1969 was thought to be over in 1970, but economic growth continued to slow because of a rise in inflation, interest rates, and unemployment. The federal deficit increased because of an increase in spending for social programs and the war in Southeast Asia. The Nixon administration attempted to evade stagflation by cutting taxes, raising interest rates, and devaluing the dollar, but these strategies were not successful.

After the US Senate stopped funding the development of the supersonic transport Boeing SST in 1971, Boeing began massive layoffs. As employees waited for pink slips, they jokingly referred to a Boeing optimist as one who brought lunch to work and a Boeing pessimist as one who left his car running in the parking lot. Out-of-work employees attempted to raise cash by placing classified ads in newspapers, but there were few buyers for their fire-sale prices on boats, cabins, and cars. Unemployment benefits were extended, federal food stamps and local food banks tried to help, yet many of the unemployed felt hopeless and committed suicide.[20]

The Nixon administration officially ended the Bretton Woods system, or "Nixon shock," on August 15, 1971. This action meant currency would no longer be backed by gold. Instead, it would be backed only by the promise of the US federal government. This action allowed the government to print more money.[21]

As housing prices dropped precipitously in 1972, my husband and I purchased our first rental property in Westlake, Ohio. It was an excellent property, yet it was many years before the property value increased.

November 1973 to March 1975
- *Type:* U-shaped stagflation recession
- *Duration:* sixteen months
- *Administrations:* Richard Nixon (resigned in 1974) and Gerald Ford
- *Notes:* OPEC and money printing were thought to be among the causes.

January 1980 to July 1980
- *Type:* First leg of W-shaped double-dip recession
- *Duration:* six months
- *Administration:* Jimmy Carter
- *Notes:* In 1979, under the Carter administration, unemployment declined to 5.6 percent, yet the economy headed to a recession.

July 1981 to November 1982
- *Type:* Second leg of W-shaped double-dip recession
- *Duration:* sixteen months
- *Administration:* Ronald Reagan
- *Notes:* The Iranian oil embargo and the unsuccessful monetary policy of Paul Volcker and the Federal Reserve were considered possible causes. The housing growth rate, steel manufacturing, and automobile production slowed. Interest rates were raised in an attempt to control inflation.

Interest rates were near 20 percent when Ronald Regan became president in January 1981. That year, John and I purchased property in California at a 13¾ percent interest rate, and we felt lucky to get the "low" rate. The property value did not increase rapidly, but as interest rates declined, we refinanced often. It is my opinion that a person should not stay out of a real-estate market simply because interest rates are high. Often properties are reduced during those times because many buyers leave the marketplace. It is wise to keep one's options open.

A bull market actually started in August 1982, but NBER did not declare the double-dip recession over until November 1982. Most investors were unaware the trend had reversed. Fearful of being caught in another market free fall, many investors remained on the sidelines, watching as profits were being made by others. In the first six months of 2013, we witnessed a similar situation. Markets were climbing yet many investors sat on the sidelines, fearful of another market crash.

By 1983, forty-nine banks had failed. In two years, eighty-nine banks failed, yet only forty-three banks failed in 1940 during the Great Depression. Since so many banks failed, it was difficult to believe the economy was in a bull market, yet the upward trend continued. Still, many investors stayed out of the market, fearing the situation would reverse.

In August 1987, those who had been anticipating a bear market were finally correct, but since they were five years late, they missed all the upside gains. This 1987 market crash began in the Far East, but the United States avoided a crisis thanks to a successful intervention by the Federal Reserve. In October 1987, the Dow dropped from 2,722 to 2,412.70. On October 19, 1987—Black Monday—the Dow plunged again to 1,738. This 22.6 percent plunge was a much larger percentage drop than the 1929 percentage drop of 12.82 percent. By 1989, the markets had rallied 40 percent.

There were many theories as to why the 1987 market crashed. Paul Tudor Jones believed it was a derivative trading problem, so he sold short. As the market declined, he covered his positions, profiting as the derivative writers were forced to sell. Seth Glickenhaus predicted the Dow would rally 40 percent after the 1987 market crash, and although it didn't come true immediately, it was considered a good prediction since it came true two years later in 1989.[22]

July 1990 to March 1991
- *Type:* V-shaped recession
- *Duration:* eight months
- *Administration:* George H. W. Bush

Bill Clinton took over as president from January 20, 1993, through January 20, 2001. In December 2000, Congress signed an economic stimulus to help the slowing economy, but a recession began three months after President Clinton left office.

March 2001 to November 2001
- *Type:* recession
- *Duration:* eight months
- *Administration:* George W. Bush
- *Notes:* On September 11, 2001, terrorists attacked the United States.[23] President Bush appeared on television appealing to Americans to help the recovery process. He suggested that shopping could help the ailing country. American women answered the call. During that time, I was living in California, and to help the cause, carloads of women got together to go into the city to shop. The economy's hard times continued, as unemployment remained a problem until June 2003.

Women were happy to be inconvenienced and shopped till they dropped to help stimulate the economy.

December 2007 to March 2009
- *Type:* L-shaped recession
- *Duration:* fifteen months
- *Administration:* George W. Bush (until January 2009), Barack Obama (January 2009 to present)

The days following this recession were similar to the volatile days after the 1929 market crash when many investors played the market aggressively and lost additional amounts of hard-earned money. In both economies, there were days the market moved higher only to retreat for longer periods of time, causing some investors to panic and sell into the lows.

The Dow closed at 13,044 on January 2, 2008, and continued to decline over the following year to a low of 6,547.05 on March 9, 2009. Lows were followed by a four-year upward trend, and if long-term investors did not purchase stocks at the lows, it was a missed opportunity. Day traders who participated in the market during the upward move may not have seen the trend evolving, since day-to-day volatility was often distracting. Markets could be higher or lower on any given day. I purchased stocks when the market hit bottom, but I often sold before much profit was made.

The recession played havoc with small-business owners. Many had to close shop. My son, Stephen, and his friend ventured into the entrepreneurial world during this recession with an innovative technology company. Although the climate for start-ups was grim, founding their company during the downturn allowed the groundwork to be laid in time for the upswing. (Their company, Framehawk, has a winning product enabling businesses to quickly and securely place any app on any mobile device or tablet, resulting in great savings of cost and time.)

The Domino Effect

When the rich cannot access cash, they pull back on making purchases, causing a ripple effect throughout the economy. Although the rich are often criticized for their success, they have made it possible for others to maintain a decent standard of living in the United States. Without the wealthy making frivolous purchases, jobs would be lost. The following examples illustrate how regular folks are affected when the rich and famous fall into hard times.

Yellowstone Club in Montana, a private ski and golf resort founded by Timothy and Edra Blixeth in 1999, employed six hundred people during its peak season. Many public figures, including Bill Gates and Dan Quayle, held memberships. The cost to join was a minimum of $250,000, and annual dues were $20,000. A 13,000-acre development surrounded the club, featuring more than eight hundred unique homes nestled in the mountains, ranging in price from $5 million to $35 million.

In 2008, Edra received the Yellowstone Resort as part of her divorce settlement along with a 249-acre estate in Rancho Mirage, California, Castle Chateau de Farcheville in Boubille, outside Paris, and an obligation to repay a $375 million loan to Credit Suisse. As the economy tanked, Edra needed to raise cash, so she placed the fifteen-bedroom, thousand-acre Castle on the market for $57 million. Although the chateau included personal hunting grounds, a helicopter pad, and its own moat, a buyer could not be found, and she was forced to file bankruptcy in March 2009 and Yellowstone also went into receivership eliminating many jobs.[24]

More jobs were lost when another billionaire, Bjorgolfur Gudmundsson, Iceland's second richest billionaire filed for bankruptcy protection in 2007. He cofounded Bravo brewery in Russia and created Botchkarov Beer. The brewery was later sold to Heineken. In 2003, Gudmundsson purchased West Ham, an English soccer team that had a value of $350 million prior to the recession. During the economic downturn, he attempted to sell the team for $200 million but was unable to raise cash. He applied for one of the largest bankruptcy-protection filings in Icelandic history.[25]

James Packer found himself in a similar situation during the recession. In 2005, Packer inherited a majority stake in PBL Media Empire Publishing and Broadcasting valued at over $7 billion. During the 2007 recession, a decrease in market value and a few bad investments cut his assets in half. Just like other billionaires who needed to free up cash, he was forced to sell some of his toys. He sold his $50 million yacht and postponed delivery of a $60 million private jet. He even stopped completion of a swimming pool.[26] Needless to say as the rich tighten their spending, jobs disappear. Given these examples, we can get an indication of what happens when wealthy investors suffer losses. Many billionaires were big winners in 2007 and 2008 but lost much of their wealth in 2009. When India's stock market fell 44 percent in 2009, Anil Ambani lost 76 percent of his wealth, or approximately $32 billion. Just a year earlier in 2008, Ambani made a profit of $24 billion. When the US economy slowed in 2009, Warren Buffett lost $25 billion. Just a year earlier, Buffett had a $10 billion profit.

During the 2009 lows, heavy losses were incurred by many billionaires, but not all investors suffered losses. Peter Kellogg, Eddie Lampert, and William Ding had some excellent gains from shares of the following companies they held from February 11, 2008, to February 13, 2009, as the chart below shows.[27]

Shareholder	Company	Price Change
Peter Kellogg	Thoratec (THOR) US medical devices	+ 84.3%
Eddie Lampert	AutoZone (AZO) US car parts	+ 16.3%
William Ding	Netease (NTES) China online gaming	+ 8.9%

Although these stocks held over the year proved successful for Kellogg, Lampert, and Ding, anyone who traded these stocks daily may not have had the same kind of profits. Daily moves were unpredictable, making it difficult for day traders to maintain profits. At times, the stock price closed down, showing a loss, yet the next day the stock price moved up. This type of volatility made it difficult for day traders to profit.

The following stocks performed well from the lows in 2008–2009:

Company	Date Purchased	Price	Date Sold	Price	% Gain
Cliffs Natural Resources, Inc.(CLF)	11/24/2008	$20.69	4/11/2011	$97.00	368.83%
Joy Global, Inc. (JOYG)	11/24/2008	$19.32	4/8/2011	$98.92	412.01%
Whole Foods Market, Inc. (WFMI)	11/24/2008	$9.97	4/1/2011	$66.73	569.31%
Apple, Inc. (AAPL)	11/24/2008	$92.95	2/17/2011	$358.30	285.48%
Oceaneering International, Inc. (OII)	11/21/2008	$21.57	4/11/2011	$85.56	296.66%
Chevron Corporation (CVX)	10/13/2008	$69.89	4/11/2011	$107.78	54.21%
Jacobs Engineering Group, Inc. (JEC)	11/6/2008	$32.70	2/18/2011	$51.55	57.65%
Caterpillar, Inc. (CAT)	2/24/2009	$26.04	4/4/2011	$113.38	335.41%

Anyone who purchased stock in the above companies during the lows in October and November 2008 and sold from February to April 2011 would have a nice profit.

Investors and traders often have opposite views of the same markets. Day traders, who are on the wrong side of a trade in the upward trend, usually have a negative outlook on the market. Long-term value investors who come into the market during the lows usually view the market as being positive.

When the US debt was downgraded from an AAA rating to an AA+ rating on August 4, 2011, the Dow dived 500 points, followed by another drop of 700 points on August 8. On August 9, the market was down again most of the day, but during the last hour of trading, the Dow made a 600-point turnaround to close up 400 points.

Four months later, in December 2011, the Dow was at 12,000, up from a low of 7,000 in March 2009, yet many investors avoided participating in the markets. NBER verified a two-year bull run, but bears disagreed with this assessment, speculating it was just a bull bounce in a bear market and the economy was headed for a double dip.

Without crystal balls, it was difficult to determine whether the bears were correct. But investors who purchased stocks at the market lows in 2009 and sold into the market highs locked in excellent gains.

> *The Dow climbed from a low of 7,000 in March 2009 to a high of 15,300 in May 2013.*

Takeaway

- Behavior analysts studying investor reactions have found both men and women react to market stimuli in a similar manner.
- Since most market technicians agree history repeats itself, learning from past experiences is an excellent way to avoid future mistakes.
- The stock market is thought to be six months ahead of where the economy is headed.
- When Kennedy got a stock tip from a shoeshine boy, he became suspicious and correctly determined the market must be oversaturated. He sold his stocks prior to the market plummeting. Was this luck or was Kennedy knowledgeable and observant?
- Markets never move in a straight line, either up or down, and during economic changes there will be more volatility than usual.

- During the evolution process, deflation, inflation, or stagflation can creep up without being noticed.
- Profits can be made in poor economic cycles by purchasing best-of-breed stocks at the lows and waiting until prices move up to sell.
- Knowing when to buy is important, but knowing when to sell can make the difference between a gain and a loss. Those who invested in GM stock in the early twenties and sold prior to the 1929 crash would have made a huge profit, but if the stock was sold after the market crash, there would have been a huge loss.
- Perception of the economy and the markets is germane to how we play the game. During the first two days after the 1929 market crash, the Dow actually closed up because of the perception provided by the White Knights. In hindsight, the worst was not over.
- A recession is most often defined as a downturn in the gross domestic product for six months or two successive quarters or more.
- Recessions are generally defined by alphabetical names, such as V-shaped, U-shaped, W-shaped, or L-shaped.
- Beware when interest rates are raised prematurely in a slowing economy.
- The Nixon administration officially ended the Bretton Woods system on August 15, 1971. This action meant currency would no longer be backed by gold and allowed the government to print more money.
- During recessions when the rich cannot access cash, they pull back on making frivolous purchases. This inaction by the rich causes a trickle-down effect in the economy.
- Since most stocks do not perform well during a recession, purchasing an excellent stock during the market lows can be quite profitable over time.

> *The market right now is moving on nothing more than emotions. Guess what? It almost always moves on emotions.*
> —*David Bach*

3

Risk vs. Reward

Emotions Rule

What prompts us to take risks? The short answer may be our emotions and our perception of the markets based on what others are doing. We generally prefer to think we are in control of our emotions, but there are times when we abandon our senses to run with the crowd. When markets are soaring, it is difficult to remain on the sidelines, so we often join with others plowing money in, causing prices to rise. We may be aware buying at new daily highs is a mistake, yet we buy anyway.

Behavior analysts have found it is human nature to run with the crowd. Studies have shown these emotions are predestined, so in order to profit, we must learn control. According to Warren Buffett, "The fact that people will be full of greed, fear, or folly is predictable. The sequence is not predictable."[28] A review of these emotions should help us determine when our investment potential may be affected. Meir Statman has found investors do better when they understand and govern their emotions and avoid acting in haste.[29]

During the 2007–2009 meltdown of the financial system, one of my friends frantically attempted to put in a sell order, but in her haste, she pressed the wrong button and instead of selling, she purchased additional shares. This turned out to be an expensive error, since the stock price continued to fall. Not to be outdone by my friend, I did something similar one day when I was multitasking. Instead of selling, I purchased additional shares of a stock I intended to sell. But in my case, by the time I noticed my error, the market had gained strength, enabling me to sell all the shares and make a profit.

Emotions Rule

Although learning to control our emotions may not be easy, it is worth the effort. Let's take a look at the emotions that steer investors wrong.

- **Fear of reentering the marketplace** often occurs after markets experience huge declines and investors incur large losses. After the market bottoms, investors choose to sit on the sidelines rather than slowly reenter the markets. Investors anticipating additional plunges will miss the largest moves from the bottom.

    Many investors missed the move when the Dow climbed from a low of 7,000 in March 2009 to a high of 12,000 in December 2011, because NBER didn't verify the two-year bull run until December 2011. The extreme volatility during the upward trend was seen by many as a gamble and not as an investment opportunity. These investors never felt comfortable participating in the markets even though profits were being made by many. Some investors believed it was a bull bounce in a bear market and the economy was headed for a double-dip recession.

    A relative of mine has been in limbo for twelve years. He owned a speculative tech stock when the bubble burst in 2001, and his stock plunged to single digits. Holding on to the stock indicates a paper loss but not a real loss, so he continues to hold the stock, waiting for the stock price to get back to even. Currently, it looks as though that stock will never return to its highs.

- **Fear of future regret** is when investors fear if they sell their loser stocks, the stocks will soar and future gains will be missed. It is

said small investors marry their losers and divorce their winners, while professionals do the opposite.
- **Greed** often coincides with the herding emotion, causing individuals to make the same stupid decisions others are making. If everyone is buying and the market is soaring, greed can cause a conservative investor to buy stocks in the final stages of an upward trend. In actuality, when stocks are at their peak, selling should be the preferred action. Being late to the party nearly always ends badly. Before the 1929 market crash, those who paid the highest prices for stock were the biggest losers.
- **Anger** often occurs after an investor encounters an unanticipated market move. It affects an investor's judgment and can cause an investor to double down or sell an entire portfolio. Even successful investors have incurred bouts of anger that cause them to make unprofitable decisions.

    In the sixties, young Warren Buffett let his anger toward a deceitful company president control an investing decision that dragged on his company for years. Buffett told viewers on CNBC he took control of the failing textile company in order to fire the president. He knew it was a bad investment, yet he allowed his anger to take control.[30]
- **Excitement** usually occurs when the market is soaring. As markets are pushed higher, the exuberance can cause conservative folks to act against their better judgment and join with others reaping monetary rewards. We find ourselves doing what others are doing, even if what they are doing is wrong.

    This emotion was strong during the Roaring Twenties, when regular folks borrowed money from their brokers and mortgaged their homes to invest in the markets. We saw it again during the tech boom, as speculators continued to jump on the bandwagon at market highs.
- **Sadness** comes in many degrees and usually follows times of exuberance. We should expect markets to decline after making purchases at the highs, yet we are surprised when the market declines. During the tech boom, stocks were soaring, yet many were surprised the bubble burst. Some investors sold after the first plunge while others waited. Many of those who waited are still holding worthless stock and are saddened they did not sell.

This extreme sadness has kept them from participating in the recent upward trend of the market. Sadness can sometimes turn into depression, so it is important to put things in the proper perspective.

The dangers of depression in this circumstance can be seen in the fate of seventy-four-year-old Adolf Merckle, once Germany's fifth richest billionaire. In late 2008, Merckle found himself in a financial crisis when his holding company, VEM Group, posted a $6 billion financial loss. In an attempt to get some quick cash, he took a short position in Volkswagen. Instead of the stock price falling as he anticipated, Porsche surprised everyone by taking a stake in VW, and the stock price made a quick reversal. This market move added another $500 million loss to Merckle's financial position.

Merckle tried various methods to obtain cash, but his attempts were unsuccessful. His creditors were unrelenting, and it became necessary to relinquish his company for $500 million. He was unable to handle this loss and committed suicide January 5, 2009, by jumping in front of an oncoming express train.[31]

- **Buyer and seller remorse** are woulda-coulda-shoulda thoughts buyers often have when stocks make unexpected moves after a purchase. Since it is nearly impossible to purchase stock at the exact bottom, it should be expected that stock prices may move lower after a purchase. In the same context, sellers often have regrets when selling too early, but it is usually better than selling late after prices plummet.
- **Regret** generally comes after making an unacceptable trade. At some time during an investor's career, a decision to purchase or sell a stock may cause regret. How this investment is handled afterward is important. Some investors will shoulder their own responsibility, while others will shift blame to financial advisors or media analysts.

The best way to proceed is to determine why the decision was made, and focus on today and the future. As Meir Statman wrote in an August 2009 *Wall Street Journal* article, "Sometimes emotions mislead us into stupid behavior. We feel the pain of regret when we find, in hindsight, that our portfolios would have been overflowing if only we had sold all the stocks in 2007."[32]

Phil Pearlman mentioned in a CNBC interview that he usually sells into upside moves and sometimes feels regret because he sells too early.[33] I made a similar mistake with Telex. It moved from single digits to double digits, and although I made a profit when I sold, I felt regret after the sell (see details in chapter 6).

- **Heartfelt feeling** is an emotion based on a personal feeling so strong we continue to follow through even though we are aware the investment will be a disaster. Many years ago, young T. Boone Pickens let his heartfelt emotion rule by purchasing a hometown company, before it went into bankruptcy. His purchase saved many jobs and he was happy to help, but by allowing his emotions to rule, the hometown purchase became a huge investment blunder.
- **Affinity of groups** is a professional term for "herding," a behavior individuals display as they join with others who follow the crowd. Many individuals feel there is safety in numbers—as in, if everyone else is doing it, it must be the correct thing to do. Investors subscribe to this theory of buying when others are buying and selling, because it makes them feel safer to be wrong with the majority than being right alone.[34]

David Dreman, investment chief of Dreman Value Management and contrarian investor, told *SmartMoney* writer Dyan Machan when he was a junior analyst in 1969, he decided to follow the crowd and invest in a skyrocketing small company with few earnings. This investment cost him 75 percent of his net worth. Dreman quit following the herd and went on a quest to find answers to why investors overpay for stocks, why they continue to make the same mistakes over and over, and why they don't learn from historical data.[35]

The price for any commodity or investment will be higher when we purchase at the same time others are making purchases. Instead of buying with others who are pushing prices higher, we should exhibit control and wait for prices to drop—just as we wait for department stores to lower their prices before we make a purchase. We are all savvy shoppers at department stores, but somehow we just can't get it right with stocks.

Truths are not always what they seem.

Supply and demand are the basic reasons stock prices move, but emotions and perception are the triggers that get us into the game. Perception of the economy has been shown to cause ordinary folks to lose their senses. When the economy is soaring and markets make new highs, ordinary folks join with others to participate in the profits, as we saw during the Roaring Twenties and the technology boom. When markets plummet, folks join with others in selling. This selling in turn causes others to sell, creating a domino effect. Often truths derived from perceptions will be inaccurate, so we must be careful. During the tech boom, many companies did not have profits, yet stock prices rose in anticipation of future profits.

What were we thinking?

Learning from mistakes is an excellent way to proceed, and I believe women are more likely to follow this strategy than men. Behavioral-finance pioneers Daniel Kahneman and Amos Tversky found some investors prefer to avoid thinking about and learning from their past mistakes. Research found many investors place a high value on loss aversion and prefer to think they are better at investing than they actually are.[36] Since men have been investing in the markets longer than women, possibly these researchers are referring to men rather than women.

As previously mentioned David Dreman[37] began to study why people continue to make the same mistakes again and again. Since our emotions affect nearly every aspect of our lives, he was not surprised to find emotions play a huge role in our investing successes and failures. It is not easy to go against what others are doing, but if having a secure future is our goal, we must learn to act independently, making observations and looking only at facts and information. His findings were similar to those of other researchers that found: [38]

- Investors generally overreact to events.
- People who run mutual funds are very much like other investors.
- If investors could overcome various biases, most mistakes could be avoided.[39]
- Preventing future mistakes can be as simple as looking at past mistakes and not repeating them.
- Less-experienced investors usually will repeat the same mistakes, but experts like Peter Lynch never make the same mistake twice.[40]

Staying in the Game

Selling or changing course in the middle of the game could be asking for trouble. If a mutual fund or stock takes a dive after you make a purchase, don't panic and change course by immediately selling. If a stock or fund is intended to be held long term, prepare for various market moves by deciding on an exit plan prior to making a purchase. Remember that value stocks, growth stocks, and mutual funds will all have low periods at various times, but in hindsight, most funds and value stocks rise over the years. Learning from the mistakes of others is less costly than learning from our own mistakes, but recently an innovative tech process has become available, making it possible to learn from our own mistakes without risk.

Hard to believe this can be true.

Kapitall, a Risk-Free Way to Learn from Mistakes

This unique gaming app developed for gamers by the genius investor Gaspard de Dreuzy encourages users to learn investing skills and participate in the market without risking real capital. Kapitall was developed as an aid for the novice investor and for anyone wishing to participate in the markets without risk. This game changer builds investment skills while minimizing the way boring statistics are presented. Since the game opened on October 14, 2010, gamers have had the opportunity to participate in an interactive setting, gaining knowledge and building skills while researching and analyzing stocks, and challenging market indexes, mutual funds, and ETFs.

> *Kapitall's goal is to make investing fun, challenging, and a rewarding experience. The site features a social-networking structure so consumers can share investing ideas with others.*[41]

John and I have accessed this unique app to check out the site and make hypothetical trades. Without putting our own money in jeopardy, we bought and sold some speculative stocks, a fun way to participate in the markets without risk. As an added benefit, this could be an interesting way to introduce the markets to our children and grandchildren.

Takeaway

- Investors take risks based on their perception of the market and what other investors are doing.
- Many emotions are triggered as markets evolve. In order to become successful, an investor must learn to control these emotions.
- When stock prices soar, investors join others making purchases at the peaks, and when prices decline, investors join the selling crowd. This action of following the herd is rarely lucrative. The best prices on best-of-breed stocks can be obtained when no one is interested in buying and the best time to sell stocks is when everyone else is buying.
- It is rarely advantageous to run with the crowd, with the possible exception of getting in at the beginning of an upward trend.
- Going against the grain can be profitable for long-term investors. Day traders should go with the flow and not "buck the trend."
- According to behavior analysts, many investor mistakes are predictable. By learning from these mistakes, we can begin to make better investing decisions.
- Allowing anger to affect an investment decision may be mentally satisfying but it can be devastating for your portfolio.
- Heartfelt emotions should not enter into investment decisions. Investors who can afford to make heartfelt investments are already successful and can do as they choose.
- Woulda-coulda-shoulda, also known as investor's remorse often comes into play after purchasing or selling a stock. After a decision is made, let it go and move on.
- Some investment rules are made to be broken. The rule to never sell at the bottom must be broken if an investor owns a speculative stock that has plummeted and it is doubtful it will ever return to its previous price.
- Kapitall, a unique investing game, can be an interesting way to build investing skills and participate in the markets without risk.

Chasing performance is the biggest mistake people make. Buying a hot fund, a fund that has already gone up, is a frequent mistake. Individuals do it overwhelmingly and consistently—it is very damaging to returns. [42]

—David Swensen

4

Game Changers

Trust Issues

Should investors go with the flow or attempt to reinvent the wheel? Some investors prefer to invest alone, just as they prefer to paint their own homes or mow their own lawns. Some do-it-yourselfers may work alone in an effort to save money, while others may have had bad experiences and do not want to repeat their mistakes. Besides cost, trust issues are a universal reason for not investing with a professional. Some investors have seen their nest egg plunge during a recession and have lost confidence in their fund manager or broker while others feel they can match the performance of professionals without paying expensive commissions. To make matters worse, many investors sold during the market lows and were out of the market during the upside moves.

Nearly all professionals bring something valuable to the table, whether it is the landscaper, the house painter, or the financial broker.

Generally, financial professionals stick to a traditional investment style unless asked for a speculative type of investment. Everyone makes errors, and investment advisors aren't any different. Considering brokers have survived various economic recessions and eventually make up their losses, I believe we can conclude most are good at what they do. As we contemplate whether to invest with a financial advisor and pay the higher commissions or trade online alone, we should consider the fact that many successful investors do not manage their own money. Commission costs may appear expensive, yet the costs of commissions ought to be inconsequential when compared to potential gains.

Having worked with a financial broker over four decades, there were times my portfolio didn't "rock," but having patience during the difficult times was an important part of the game.

For the best possible results with minimum effort, finding an excellent broker in a full-service firm and investing slowly may be in your best interest. Firms prosper in the good times and are able to handle slow economies. The following data demonstrates how four investment firms handled the slowing economy from 2009 to 2011.

Raymond James

Brokers: In 2009, the firm had 5,000 brokers; by 2011, it had 4,500 brokers (decrease).

Branches: In 2009, the firm had 2,280 branches; by 2011, it had 1,600 branches (decrease).

UBS

Brokers: In 2009, the firm had 13,900 brokers; by 2011, it had 6,800 brokers (decrease).

Branches: In 2009, the firm had 720 branches; by 2011, it had 300 branches (decrease).

Edward Jones

Brokers: In 2009, the firm had 12,000 brokers; by June 2011, it still had all 12,000 brokers (no change).

Branches: In 2009, the firm had 10,880 branches; by 2011, it had 11,000 branches (increase).[43]

Merrill Lynch

Brokers: In 2009, the firm had 15,000 brokers; by 2011, it had 13,900 brokers (decrease).

Branches: In 2009, the firm had 790 branches; by 2011, it had 700 branches (decrease).[44]

The brokerage houses mentioned above made many changes during the 2007 recession to become leaner and more focused. It is my opinion most brokers will do a good job if we give them the opportunity by keeping our accounts open. During difficult times when stock prices decline, less experienced investors sell or close their accounts, causing a domino effect in the markets. Instead of selling and pushing prices lower, an investor should be looking for an entry point into the market.

Shopping for a Financial Advisor

Blindly picking a financial broker from the list of 500,000 investment professionals available in the United State can be disconcerting. It's much easier if you ask friends, relatives, or colleagues if they are satisfied with their financial advisor and whether they would recommend his or her services. Financial brokers from reputable firms usually have a particular strategy that works for them, and it's prudent to select a broker whose philosophy is a good match for yours. Most brokers take into consideration many things about each client before they begin investing. Some financial advisors make recommendations but will not do whatever a client wishes. My broker was spot-on when it came to selecting stocks, and he had no problem allowing me to select some stocks on my own.

Financial Industry Regulatory Authority (FINRA) keeps a file on each licensed financial professional in the United States. Most reputable firms will not hire a broker with any sort of black mark on their record.[45] Selecting a financial advisor who works for a large firm may give you fewer sleepless nights, but it doesn't guarantee the results will be financially favorable. Some investors prefer to work with an independent advisor, who may be more amenable to their wishes than a financial broker. Although most financial advisors work alone, they may have a support team. Use their past record as a reference point, but remember that past performance does not guarantee future results. Many advisors are interested in offering annuities to new clients. As we know, not all annuities are for everyone, so if you feel inclined to go down that path, it is best to investigate both the annuity and the advisor before turning over any cash.

One former independent investment advisor in the news during the past few years is Bernard "Bernie" Madoff. He is now serving time at Butner Federal Correctional Institution for fraud and other charges, including false filings with the SEC and theft from an employee benefit plan. Madoff said he began his Ponzi scheme in the early 1990s, but some believe the operation was never legitimate and fraud began as early as the 1980s. The amount missing from clients' accounts is thought to be approximately $65 billion.

Online Sites for Checking Out Financial Advisors

Before investing with a financial advisor, always do a thorough check. Besides asking friends or relatives for opinions, the following online resources can help you find out the status of a financial advisor.

- FINRA (Financial Industry Regulatory Authority)
  http://www.finra.org
- EDGAR (Electronic Data Gathering, Analysis, and Retrieval System)
  http://www.sec.gov/edgar.shtml
- NAPFA (National Association of Personal Finance Advisors)
  http://www.napfa.org

Speculative Stocks

Brokers recommend products they think can make the most money in the shortest amount of time, but sometimes these products do not perform as intended. Hard-to-understand products should be avoided, because buying these may be detrimental to your portfolio. Brokers who recommended auction rate securities (ARS) unintentionally put their clients in a difficult position. Invented by Ronald Gallatin at Lehman Brothers around 1984, ARS were introduced by Goldman Sachs in 1988. This corporate or municipal bond had a long-term maturity with an interest rate reset regularly through a Dutch auction.

Many investors bought ARS under the impression they were as liquid as cash. This supposition should have been accurate, but because of certain unforeseen conditions, the securities turned out to be a disaster.[46] In 2008, the auction markets were abandoned by the banks, causing a freeze. This left investors without access to their cash.

When retired Bill Reid Jr. purchased the ARS, he found it difficult to understand but was told the debt instruments were as safe as a money market fund. A year after the market froze, he still had tens of thousands of dollars locked up in those securities. He did not know when his money would be returned to him.[47]

Even the most elite investors can get duped. Robert Citron, a conservative investor and the treasurer and tax collector for Orange County, California, fell for one of these risky investments when he tried to make up for losses in tax revenue after Proposition 13 passed and less money was coming into the county. At first, Citron's investments made substantial profits, and he was considered a hero—but as the economy slowed, his gain turned into a $1.7 billion loss. Orange County had to file for bankruptcy protection in 1994.[48]

Mutual Funds

Every investment carries some degree of risk, and mutual funds are no exception. In *The Unofficial Guide to Investing*, published in 1999, Lynn O'Shaughnessy wrote that a case could be made that mutual funds are safer than banks and savings and loans, since not one mutual fund had gone under since the passage of the Federal Investment Company Act in 1940.[49] At the time of her writing, she was correct—but since then, Lehman Brothers and Bear Stearns have set a new precedent. As a result, managed funds may appear less desirable to low-risk investors.

When mutual funds were first introduced in the 1960s, most of them did not perform well, but T. Rowe Price's portfolios were successful because his fund invested in growth stocks. At that time, savings accounts had better returns than funds composed of stocks and bonds. Price's investments did well, yet his employees bought him out in the midsixties.[50]

Reading the Prospectus

Anyone contemplating the purchase of a mutual fund should read the entire prospectus, since it is the formal legal agreement between the investor and the fund company. The prospectus contains information about the fund's objectives, its investment strategies, the types of stock it owns, and the risks associated with the investment. It also includes the distribution policy, the fund's management style, and its fees and expenses.

The market value of a mutual fund is based on all the securities the fund owns, plus the cash it holds, minus any expenses. Fund prices fluctuate as prices of the stocks held by the fund increase or decrease in value. The net asset value (NAV) is the price we pay when we buy or sell a mutual fund. This price quote can be found at the end of the day. Any capital gains, dividends, and interest paid to the fund are distributed to the fund owners as per law. Taxes on gains must be paid by fund holders regardless of whether the account made or lost money. In addition to any upfront fees, a yearly management fee is charged on the NAV of each fund owner regardless of whether the fund generates gains or sustains losses. Although there are many costs associated with owning a mutual fund, if history is any indication of the future, the gains will trivialize the management costs. Though past fund performance may not be indicative of future performance, successes or failures can be used as a point of reference.

There are many ways to invest in mutual funds. Some investors like to time the market by adding money to brokerage accounts when prices are low. When an entire sector is declining, even excellent stocks in that sector will fall. Stock prices moving lower because of sector unpopularity or for reasons other than financials generally will increase in value over time. If you are a value investor, you may choose to purchase funds with best-of-breed companies in an unpopular sector during price declines. Purchasing more of a fund you already own as it declines will provide a lower base price. If timing the market is difficult, some professionals recommend buying shares of funds in increments on a regular basis. The base price may be somewhat higher, but stressful decisions can be avoided while still dollar-cost averaging.

There are various ways to take advantage of dollar-cost averaging. If we want to be in control, we can buy on days when the market is down. If we want to take responsibility out of the equation, we can relieve ourselves of blame and regret when things go badly by buying at a predetermined time each month whether the prices are high or low. Another way is to make a purchase on a certain day each month when the market is down. Some professionals suggest dividing the amount of money we have to invest into ten equal trades. Select a date and invest the amount on that date each month for ten months. This minimizes regret if the market declines after the first investment. If the market rises, it is comforting that some of our investment is working for us. This procedure works for any amount we have to invest:

- $100,000 divided into 10 trades equal $10,000 to be invested each month for ten months
- $50,000 divided into 10 trades equal $5,000 to be invested each month for ten months
- $25,000 divided into 10 trades equal $2,500 to be invested each month for ten months
- $10,000 divided into 10 trades equal $1,000 to be invested each month for ten months
- $5,000 divided into 10 trades equal $500 to be invested each month for ten months
- $1,000 divided into 10 trades equal $100 to be invested each month for ten months

Before investing in any mutual fund, it is essential to research fund history and performance, yet past performance may not be indicative of the future because of certain economic conditions that exist or contribute to the success or failure of the fund in any particular year. There are many funds available in various sectors, ranging from small-cap companies to large-cap companies. Each fund has a specific, defined investment goal, and the stocks they represent are all geared toward that objective. Prices differ for these funds, so it is necessary to explore all available options before committing to any particular one. In 2007, there were more than six thousand mutual funds—most of them similar, with slightly different objectives.

Mutual funds can be classified into some of the following categories: growth, balanced, bond/income, and money market. These main categories can also be divided into subcategories. The following examples offer some insight.

Growth Mutual Funds

There are many different kinds of growth mutual funds:

- **Single-asset mutual funds** purchase stock in one particular industry, such as gold, banking, or pharmaceuticals. They are riskier than owning stocks in diversified sectors. They can be a lucrative investment or a huge disappointment, depending on the timing, the market, and the structure of the purchase.

My husband and I owned two single-asset mutual funds: a gold fund in the eighties that should have been a winner and a risky speculative technology fund in the nineties. Our technology fund was purchased in increments over time as prices were declining. After we were all in, investors began anticipating a profitable future and prices began to rise. As the news hit the front pages and the general public became aware of the upward moves, many who had never invested in the markets hopped on the bandwagon, causing prices to go higher. As prices soared, exuberance was everywhere. After the market was saturated, we sold into the highs. This turned out to be an excellent strategy. As we know from hindsight, the bubble burst in 2001 and tech prices plummeted. Anyone who did not take profits prior to the market decline sustained huge losses. Many investors and mutual-fund managers treated the pullback as a market correction and not a market crash. Although we exited this mutual fund, I continued to trade two other tech stocks, buying on the dips and selling as the prices reversed. This worked well until the market began diving and I continued to add to my positions.

Not only did I misread the signals, many investors and mutual-fund managers misread the seriousness of the tech decline and losses were huge. The Internet Kinetics Asset Management Fund managed by Ryan Jacob was the best-performing mutual fund in 1998, with an approximate gain of 196 percent. After the tech bubble burst in 2001, Jacob's new fund, the Jacob Internet Fund, was down 66 percent. He noted in a letter to his shareholders that his biggest mistake was reacting to the sell-off as a market correction when in fact it was a market crash.[51]

The gold fund I purchased should have been a winner, but I made two critical mistakes during the purchasing process, and it turned out to be a huge loser (see chapter 8 for details).

- **Large-capitalization growth mutual funds** have a market value of $12 billion or more. Investing in large-cap mutual funds represents less risk, but returns will be lower. These funds are less volatile because they invest in companies with market values of $8 billion to $10 billion.

- **Mid-capitalization growth mutual funds** have a market value between $1 billion and $12 billion. In the early seventies, my husband and I began investing monthly in a mid-cap growth mutual fund. The fund price continued to plummet after we made our initial purchase, but we continued to invest the same amount monthly. By the midseventies, the market appeared to bottom, and we were still onboard. Selling at the bottom and watching the stock rise is not a winning strategy, so we continued investing monthly, effectively dollar-cost averaging. After prices began rising and we passed the break-even point, we sold our shares, locking in a small profit. Since another market plunge could not be ruled out, we felt it was in our best interest to take the small profit. In hindsight, the market and the fund price continued to soar without us.

    A better strategy would have been to invest additional money into the fund at the lows and hold the fund long-term.
- **Small-cap growth mutual funds** invest in equity shares of smaller companies with the hope of reaping dividends when the businesses reach their full potential.
- **Emerging-market growth mutual funds** invest in developing regions of the world where stocks are generally not expensive but extremely volatile. In 1993, the emerging markets posted an excellent return of nearly 75 percent. The following year, the emerging markets plunged below 7 percent.

    Needless to say, one must be very careful and selective in this market.
- **International growth mutual funds** invest in securities of foreign corporations. The typical fund represents stocks in established countries having blue-chip stocks like Sony or Toyota.
- **Global growth mutual funds** invest in securities of US corporations as well as foreign corporations.
- **Aggressive growth mutual funds** invest in less well-known securities in an attempt to make larger profits. These funds are very risky, but the reward can be substantial if the company succeeds.

    You should avoid aggressive funds if you want a safe investment.
- **Value mutual funds** invest in large-cap and medium-cap companies paying above-average dividends and offering value when compared to similar companies.

Balanced Mutual Funds

There are two kinds of balanced mutual funds:

- **Traditional balanced mutual funds** invest in relatively conservative blends of stocks, bonds, and money-market instruments. They tend to have less volatility than a portfolio made up of only stocks.
- **Asset-allocation funds** invest in a mix of stocks, bonds, and money-market instruments, but as market conditions change, these funds switch the percentage of their holdings. They are more volatile than the traditional balanced mutual fund.

Bond or Income Mutual Funds

With these investments, you are investing in either bonds or high-paying dividend stocks. Their objective is to provide income to investors.

Money Market Mutual Funds (MMFs)

MMFs invest in short-term liquid debt instruments normally offering higher interest rates than a checking or savings account. Technically, money markets are not as safe as bank deposits like CDs, because they are not insured by the FDIC. That being said, historically they have proved to be a relatively safe investment. MMFs can be any of the following:

- **Active managed mutual funds** usually keep twenty-five to fifty stocks in their portfolio. Managers do hands-on research and purchase stocks without any input from their clients. A fee is charged for this type of fund. Some believe these funds will become obsolete since they are unable to beat the market. It is believed that index funds and ETFs provide broader asset class diversification at lower prices.[52]
- **Index mutual funds** are a passive type of managed fund. Managers purchase the stock of an entire index. In the late nineties, when the markets were booming, the mutual funds duplicating the

S&P 500 saw some excellent returns. During the 1991 recession, my husband and I began purchasing an equity index mutual fund in monthly increments. As the price continued to decline, we continued to invest. After the recession ended, the fund price began to rise, and it continued to climb for approximately ten years, at which time we moved the winning index fund into another fund. Purchasing an equity index fund in a bear market has the potential for maximum growth because fund prices are lowest at that time, and eventually, as the economic situation improves, fund prices usually accelerate. Timing is always important, so it would be preferable to purchase an index fund at the end of a bear market or the beginning of a bull market. Without a crystal ball, that is often a difficult feat. Holding on to a fund as it is decelerating can be a nail-biting process, but if history is our guide, this too will pass.

- **Exchange-traded funds (ETFs)** became available in the United States in 1993 and in Europe in 1999. ETFs combine features of mutual funds with features of stocks. ETFs track an index like mutual funds, but unlike mutual funds, they can be bought and sold throughout the day like a stock. When buying an ETF, you are buying units of ownership in a trust that holds either shares of stock or bonds of a particular index. As with stocks and mutual funds, there are risks involved. By owning an ETF, you get the diversification of an index fund as well as the ability to sell short, buy on the margin, or purchase as little as one share. When buying and selling an ETF, you pay the same commission to your broker as on any regular stock order.
- **Load mutual funds** charge a fee either on the front end or the back end of a transaction. The front-end load fund was the first type of fund offered, and later the back-end loaded fund became popular due mainly to employer sponsorship. In these cases, the fees of the back-end loaded fund were usually waived. Currently, many financial managers are recommending no one should purchase a mutual fund with a yearly fee higher than 1 percent. Practically all load funds charge annual distribution fees, known as *12b-1 fees*, which are used to pay for promotional costs. Front-end load funds charge a sales fee on the initial purchase as well as on every subsequent transaction. Back-end load funds do not have

an upfront commission charge, but a maintenance or percentage fee is charged at the time the money is withdrawn from the fund. If the fund is held approximately ten years or more, the fees may be waived. Research shows load funds do not outperform no-load funds, as was previously believed.

In the slowing economy of the early seventies, with declining housing values and lower stock prices, our cousin Larry began investing in a front-end loaded mutual fund and convinced us to do likewise. This was our first front-end loaded fund, so we were not certain what to expect. We followed his lead and committed to a ten-year program. After making an initial down payment, we were obligated to invest a specific amount of money monthly for ten years. The broker retained a 5 percent fee out of each monthly payment, and the remainder was applied to purchasing shares of the fund. As the market continued to decline, our monthly payments remained the same, but we received more shares of the fund.

After a few years of declining prices and loss of value, Larry sold his shares, locking in a substantial loss. He deposited the same amount of cash monthly into a safe investment vehicle with the intention of reentering the equities market in the future. We continued investing in the fund even though we had no way of knowing when prices would begin to stabilize or improve.

Our dividends and monthly investment increased the number of shares we owned, yet after ten years of investing, our account value was less than the amount we invested. The high cost of fees and the decrease in market value contributed to our loss. Since our ten-year obligation was over, we had the option of cashing out or letting the investment ride. Since we didn't want to invest any additional money into the fund, we just let it ride. Then, as if by magic, the bulls took over and instead of the fund price continuing to decline, the asset value began to improve and the fund continued to grow over the next twenty years.

Although this fund turned from a major loser into an enormous winner, our return would have been much larger if the 5 percent monthly fee had been applied as part of the investment.

During this same time frame, Larry was still waiting for the proper time to invest his savings in equities. His nest egg was secure and liquid, yet the return on his savings couldn't keep up with our fund's rewarding performance.

- **No-load mutual funds** have no sales fees. Some no-load funds charge 12b-1 fees, but true no-load funds or 100 percent no-load funds do not charge 12b-1 fees.
- **Open-end mutual funds** have no limit on the number of shares a fund can issue and sell. Most mutual funds are open-ended.
- **Closed-end mutual funds** determine the number of shares available at the opening. After the predetermined number of shares have been sold, no other shares will be sold unless shareholders sell their shares. Closed-end mutual funds are not as popular as open-end mutual funds.

Check Out Mutual Funds before Investing

Before purchasing a mutual fund, check the rankings of each fund against other funds. Also check out the top ten holdings in each fund. These online resources can help:

- Morningstar: Evaluates and ranks many funds
  http://www.morningstar.com
- SmartMoney: Specialty search tools
  http://www.smartmoney.com
- CNN Money: Fund articles and tools
  www.mfmag.com
- Advisor One: Search for information
  http://www.advisorone.com
- Yahoo! Finance: Search finance information
  http://www.finance.yahoo.com

Mutual Fund Jargon

Knowledge relating to the markets and professional lingo can be very helpful when speaking with a broker or professional analyst. If you choose to invest with a full-service investment broker, it is wise to pay attention to monthly statements so you get a better understanding of how your investment compares to various indexes. Brokers may not always have winning stock picks, but we can get an indication of whether or not we should continue to invest with the professional.

- **12b-1 fee** is an operational fee expense. Currently the only funds that do not add this fee are 100 percent no-load funds.
- **A shares** are front-end loaded mutual funds.
- **Advisor fee** is an upfront fee an investor pays on A shares. The fee usually starts around 4 to 5 percent, but as additional money is invested, the percentage may decrease.
- **Cash reserve** is the amount of cash kept in the mutual fund. A fund with a substantial amount of cash is not fully invested and has the ability to purchase additional stocks.
- **Dollar-cost averaging** occurs when more of a stock we already own is purchased as the price drops, giving us a lower base price.
- **Expense ratio** affects our rate of return.
- **Fund yield** is the dividend the fund pays to the investor at the end of the year.
- **Morningstar rating** is a premium rating for mutual funds.
- **Net asset value (NAV)** is the price quoted at the end of the day and the price we pay or receive when we buy or sell a mutual fund.
- **Prospectus** is a formal legal document between the investor and the fund. We should always read it, since it gives all the information about the fund.
- **Risk rating** is done by Morningstar. Companies do not pay for ratings.
- **Return on Investment (ROI)** refers to the gains we receive on our investment.
- **Securities and Exchange Commission (SEC)** is a federal agency that helps with fraud encounters.

- **Year-to-date (YTD)** is the period starting from the beginning of the current year on January 1 and continuing to the present day.

Takeaway

- Investment advisors offer many perks and may be worth the commission they charge.
- Finding an investment advisor can be as easy as asking a friend or colleague for a referral.
- When selecting an investment advisor, it is best to choose one who is a good match with your own investing style.
- Some financial advisors have their own style. Some will offer recommendations, while others will make investing decisions without any input from the client.
- Since timing the market is not an easy endeavor, purchasing stocks in increments over time is the best strategy. Most financial advisors will recommend this type of investing.
- Beware of unscrupulous advisors. There are many excellent ones, but as in other avenues of life, there are a few bad apples. Check with friends and relatives as well as some of the websites available before turning over your money to an advisor.
- Buying speculative stocks is generally not a good idea for a long-term investor. Day traders can work with spec stocks and make some excellent profits if they are careful.
- Hard-to-understand products should be avoided. If a security is difficult to understand, do not get involved.
- An example of a hard-to-understand product is the auction rate security (ARS). These debt securities are sold through a Dutch auction at the lowest possible yield. Although the security is a long-term debt, it acts as if it were shorter term since rates are reset approximately every month.
- Anyone contemplating the purchase of a mutual fund should read the entire prospectus since it is the formal legal agreement between the investor and the fund company. It is important to understand the specifics of the fund before investing.

- Before investing in any mutual fund, it is essential to research fund history and performance, yet it is important to note past performance may not be indicative of the future.
- There are many different kinds of growth mutual funds. Before purchasing a mutual fund, check the rankings of each fund against other funds. Also check out the top ten holdings in each fund.
- There are load funds and no-load funds. No-load funds have become quite popular because there are no upfront fees. The entire investment amount is used for purchasing fund shares.
- Research shows load funds do not outperform no-load funds, as was previously believed.
- Timing the purchase of a mutual fund makes sense. Buying into a mutual fund at the market lows, after the fund price has declined, is a good strategy.
- Purchasing a speculative fund may or may not be a very rewarding experience. Although larger risks equal larger rewards, sometimes a speculative purchase may end in failure.
- Taxes on mutual funds must be paid whether a portfolio makes money or loses money. The taxes are based on dividends the fund receives from investments throughout the year.

Character and intelligence of the owner or company executives is more important than flash and money spending habits.

—Bill Gross

5

Confessions of the Rich and Famous

Market Blunders and Straight Talk

Why do I buy high and sell low when I know success will only come to those who do the opposite? Investors have been struggling with this question for decades. Those who solve this mystery have gone on to be successful, while others are still repeating mistakes and supporting losses. In the past, when my investments consisted of mostly value stocks, the daily volatility had little impact on my portfolio—but as a day trader, the daily swings make the difference between success and failure. As we look at those who are successful, we find most are long-term investors, and day-trading is not a part of their investment platform.

When it comes to selecting a stock for the long term, most investors look at company financials, yet most money managers agree another important ingredient in the selection process should be the management team. Warren Buffett has shared the following about employees, but the same could be said for management: "Company employees must possess three qualities: integrity, intelligence, and energy. If they don't have the first, the other two will kill you."[53]

Bill Gross, PIMCO cochief and bond-fund manager, shared a few of the lessons he learned early in his career with viewers on CNBC's "Squawk Box."[54] Since company financials are significant to an investor, other key parts are sometimes ignored as in the following examples:

- Although company financials are a priority, the managerial team is what makes or breaks a company. Top management sets the tone for the entire company; managers can take a mediocre company and make it into an exceptional company or they can bring a good company to its knees—just as top executive Dennis Kozlowski did at Tyco International. Kozlowski equated success with extravagance and took company funds for his personal use. It's rumored he spent $6,000 for a floral shower curtain for his New York apartment. He was found guilty of fraud and grand larceny and is presently serving jail time.[55]
- Character of the management team is important. In the early seventies, when Warren Buffett and Charlie Munger applied for a $10 million loan from Gross and PIMCO, they were turned down based on their collateral not complying with company standards. These two gentlemen proceeded to borrow money from Pacific Mutual and structured Berkshire Hathaway, now employing over 200,000 people.
- Truths and realism are not always evident. Not only were Buffet and Munger denied a loan from PIMCO, Sam Walton was also denied a loan. Walton wanted to expand into Iowa and Ohio but was unable to convince Gross and PIMCO he was an excellent risk. He went on to borrow millions from Pacific Mutual and established Sam's and Walmart.
- What you see may not be what you get. After Buffett, Munger, and Walton were all denied loans, Itel (not Intel) applied for a multimillion dollar loan. Their presentation was impressive, and PIMCO's Gross decided Itel's assets and top management withstood the PIMCO standards test. Six months after receiving a substantial loan, the company failed.

> *Beware of smoke-and-mirrors presentations. Flash meant to impress may lack character.*

As Bill Gross learned, it is not always easy to spot winners or losers, and truth may not be what it seems. The men who were not given loans went on to become successful, while the company that appeared to be the real deal failed.

What You Can Learn from the Rich

Investors have learned over the years that value stocks are slow movers but increase over time. In 1928, investing in value stocks was nothing more than a theory when Benjamin Graham began teaching this prototype at Columbia Business School. As the model grew in popularity, many found that although there is always risk to investing, value stocks take away some of the risk since they are slow movers and reasonably safe.

Graham believed stock owners should not be too concerned about how the stock market moves short-term.[56] Investors were able to test this theory when the market crashed the following year in 1929. Although it was difficult to determine which stocks were actually value stocks and great bargains, investors looked for successful companies with a lot of cash that had been driven down for no reason other than sellers needing to access cash.

Eventually, Graham became known as the Father of Value Investing. He had four protégées who not only studied under him but worked on Wall Street during the 1929 market crash and survived various other bull and bear markets. Some say it was luck. Some say it was opportunity knocking, as in being at the right place at the right time. In any case, these four successful men—Walter Schloss, Seth Glickenhaus, Irving Kahn, and Warren Buffett—knew how to take advantage of opportunity. We can learn much from the strategies they used and their take on the countless economies they survived.

> **Definition of Luck**
> *The harder you work, the luckier you get.*

The following information was obtained from interviews these men gave Reshma Kapadia following some of the worst market moves in 2007 through 2009. In addition to managing their own portfolios, they were still managing money for clients at the time of the 2009 interviews.[57]

Walter Schloss, having lived through many economic cycles, found that when stock prices plummeted, it was a buying opportunity. The veteran stock analyst told Kapadia that dividends were the primary reason regular folks invested in the markets during the Great Depression. He explained rents were approximately $32 per month, and American Telephone and Telegraph paid an annual dividend of $9 per share. Depending on how many shares a person owned, the dividend went a long way toward paying the rent. Schloss saw the following similarities and differences between what had been happening during 2007–2009 and what had happened back in the 1930s.

- Back in the thirties, during the Depression, bank chiefs were hauled before Congress just as they had been during the 2007–2009 recession.
- Fraud was prevalent back then, as it has been recently. The president of the New York Stock Exchange was accused of fraud, and regulators were considering a ban on short-selling.
- Presently, many regular folks own stock in their IRAs and Roths, whereas during the thirties, only 10 percent of the population was invested in stocks. At that time, financial news rarely made the front page, while nowadays we are constantly inundated with market information.
- In the past, the economy was dependent on just a few businesses, while currently we have many powerful industries that should provide a wider array of job possibilities and more growth for our economy.
- The situation during the 2007–2009 recession was not as dire as during the Great Depression.[58]
- Investors, having fewer emotions during the market lows in 2009, could see it was a buying opportunity, just as investors who invested during the market lows in the thirties.[59]

Seth Glickenhaus, veteran investor and municipal-bond trader at Salomon Brothers during the Great Depression, related a true story to Kapadia about how his bosses at Salomon Brothers rejected a recommendation he made concerning newly issued Arkansas state bonds. Glickenhaus suggested these bonds should be a good investment, since the state defaulted on its debt and was near bankruptcy. Since Glickenhaus was unable to convince his bosses, they took a pass, and another investor made a fortune on the investment while Glickenhaus and Salomon missed out.

Irving Kahn, a veteran money manager, told Kapadia he was viewing the 2009 crisis differently than younger investors. Three of his theories:

- Even though stocks fell 40 percent in 2008, the worst annual return since 1937, there were so many differences in how the Fed handled the circumstances that it would be impossible to repeat the thirties.
- In past economies, the Federal Reserve wasn't able to lend money unless it was backed by gold, whereas since 1971, the government was able to keep the economy on track by creating billions of dollars.
- Lower interest rates and other programs are in place to help keep individuals from sustaining the huge losses that happened in the thirties.[60]

Warren Buffett, the Berkshire Hathaway guru, often stresses the virtues of long-term investing. Value investors buy for the long term and do not make rash decisions, even if they miss out on a rock-bottom price. Although Buffett often refers to the stocks he buys as cheap, he does not buy cheap stocks.[61] It has been said if a person invested $10,000 with Buffett in 1956, the investment would be worth approximately $80 million thirty years later.[62] Two other value investors who made huge profits for their clients over the years are John Neff, retired Vanguard Windsor Value fund manager, and George Soros of Soros's Quantum Fund.

John Neff told Dyan Machan in 2006 he considered Citigroup a value play, since it had been beaten up in the early nineties. In hindsight, we know that unless Citigroup was sold before the stock took a dive, reaching a low of $1.78 per share on March 9, 2009, his profit would have turned into a huge loss. Citigroup shares are still hovering around $4.50 a share. The company has announced a reverse stock split of one share for each ten shares outstanding. It will reduce the number of shares outstanding from 25 billion to 2.9 billion. It has been said Neff's Vanguard Windsor Fund had a 5,546 percent return between 1964 and 1995, indicating that a $10,000 investment in 1964 would have been worth over a half million dollars by 1995, more than double the S&P 500.[63]

George Soros is a successful investor who no longer manages clients' money. It has been rumored that Soros's Quantum Fund returned his investors an average of 31 percent each year from 1969 to 2000, and that investing $10,000 in Soros's Quantum Fund in 1969 and selling it in 2000 would have resulted in an approximate return of $43 million.[64]

David Dreman's studies found low price/earnings (P/E) stocks outperformed high P/E stocks over time. If $1 million had been invested in low P/E ratio stocks in 1970, the earnings would have grown to approximately $228 million by late 2000, while investing $1 million in high P/E ratio stocks would have earned only $23 million during the same time frame.[65]

Fear of the Wall Street Cockroach

Professionals often react differently to market stimuli than small investors. One difference is that professionals fear the "Wall Street cockroach," and most small investors do not share this fear. Conventional wisdom is that when you see one cockroach, there are probably many others that you cannot see; the cockroach theory in investing equates this with problems on company reports. Disappointing earnings in one quarter are generally followed by more disappointing reports. Worried Wall Street professionals run for the exits immediately, while small investors wait to see what the next report will show.

Roger Stamper has said, "Even if we have to take a 30 percent loss, we'll get out. It's the cockroach theory. I've seen too many times when you wait around a quarter or two to see if the company improves, and it just gets worse."[66] According to William Berger, "We think one surprise may beget another surprise, so we get rid of the stock."[67]

Many professionals and small investors presently own the popular Apple computer stock. On July 25, 2011, Apple reported a disappointing financial number. The price fell from $600.92 to $574.88. Will Wall Street professionals react to this company report as they do with other companies and run for cover, or will they agree with those who believe this is different? The close on August 1, 2012, was $606.81. On August 22, 2012, Apple closed at $668.87. On February 21, 2013, Apple closed at $446.06. On April 18, 2013, Apple closed at $392.05. It looks as though the Wall Street cockroach has infected the Apple.

George Vanderheiden has said, "As soon as I see the first crack, I get out. I want to sell my mistakes quickly. If I buy a stock thinking the company's new concept will do well, and it doesn't work out, I'll sell. Usually the first piece of bad news is not the last piece of bad news."[68]

Takeaway

- Besides looking at company financials, it is important to look at the managerial team. Those at the top can make or break a company.
- Beware of smoke and mirrors. Companies may use flash in an attempt to impress.
- During the market lows in 2009, value investors could see it was a buying opportunity just as investors who invested during the market lows in the thirties.
- Father of Value Investing Benjamin Graham believed stock owners should not be too concerned about how the stock market moves short-term.
- Value investors use the strategy of selecting stocks trading for less than their intrinsic value. In other words, the value investor buys excellent stocks at low prices and holds them long-term until they increase in value.
- Warren Buffett often refers to the stocks he buys as cheap, meaning he buys when the price of expensive stocks are cheap. He does not buy cheap stocks.
- David Dreman's studies found low price/earnings (P/E) stocks outperformed high P/E stocks over time.
- Luck is often equated with success, yet many know the harder we work, the luckier we get.
- Fear of the Wall Street cockroach originates from the "cockroach theory": If you see one cockroach, there are many more you cannot see. Wall Street fears once a company issues a poor financial report, it will be followed by more poor financial reports in the future. Professionals equating this situation to cockroaches will cut and run immediately.

> *When markets decline, long-term investors look for best-of-breed stocks with a low price/earnings ratio.*

Risk and return go together. So, if you think the market is risky today, then you should also think the market has a good potential for high returns.[69]

—*Meir Statman*

6

The Inside Scoop

Long-term investors have a different philosophy than day traders. Long-term investors invest in the future of a company for as long as they own the stock, while day traders look for a company with little regard for the value of the company; generally, they buy and sell the stock on the same day. Since my investment strategy was similar to the Buffett style of investing during my early years in the marketplace, many of my friends find it curious that I became an obsessive day trader after spending more than four decades in the long-term investment arena. Warren Buffett claims mistakes are part of the game, and since day-trading is more hands-on than investing for the long term, it should be no surprise day traders make more mistakes than long-term investors.[70]

The Art of Investing

Long-term investors look forward to huge market plunges, as equity investments have proved to be an excellent opportunity for future monetary gain. Investors generally look for best-of-breed stocks based on subjective, intrinsic, or actual value of the security. Buying habits are similar to how women shop department-store sales, trying to get the best-value merchandise at the lowest sale prices.

Companies may be undervalued for reasons other than financials. Stock prices move up and down in conjunction with daily news or a rumor, resulting in a price movement not corresponding with the company's long-term fundamentals. Sometimes an entire sector comes under attack, and excellent stocks in the sector get punished. When the Dow plummeted, October 19, 1987, many long-term investors purchased best-of-breed stocks. This was one of the largest one-day point drops in history. Investors referred to this day as Black Monday because the market plunged 554 points in just a few hours. Some investors panicked and sold while others used it as a buying opportunity.

Another example of a buying opportunity occurred April 15, 2013, when the market was sluggish because gold was selling off. At approximately three p.m., two bombs exploded at the finish line of the Boston Marathon; the Dow dropped 250 points to 14,599, the NASDAQ dropped 76 points to 3,216, and the Russell 2000 dropped 35 points to 907. Many folks were hurt, and others lost their lives in the explosion. Those who took advantage of the market lows during the atrocious tragedy have seen their investment grow.

Five Investment Strategies for Long-Term Investors

- Avoid premarket purchases unless there is news that makes a stock take a temporary plunge. If a market is climbing, it's best to wait for a decline to make a purchase. The market usually will decline after a major rally, giving the investor an opportunity to buy.
- Before making a purchase, evaluate stocks according to risk/reward. If a stock trading at $20 per share is determined to be $29 per share on the upside and $17 dollars a share on the downside; the risk/reward would be $9 to $3. This is a good risk/reward ratio, since the upside risk is three times the downside risk. If that stock goes up to $24 per share, the risk/reward becomes less attractive; the risk is $5 on the upside and $7 on the downside.
- Consider eliminating a stock from your portfolio if it or the sector fails to perform during a major market rally. This usually means the stock is a dud.

- If the term "restructuring" is associated with a company correcting mistakes, it should be considered a red flag, and selling may be a good strategy.
- Purchasing stocks with dividends is usually an excellent strategy.[71]

> *Since long-term investors do not sell often, it may be cost-effective to work with a full-service firm. In addition to getting an expert advisor, full-service firms provide various perks unavailable to online traders.*

Effects of Economic News

Economic news keeps the markets moving. As unbelievable as it may seem, markets need both positive and negative input to stay on track.

There are many sources of information available to help traders make informed decisions. Brokerage firms and independent brokers offer subscription newsletters, and *Fortune* or *Forbes* magazines can be purchased, as well as newspapers like *Barrons* and the *Wall Street Journal*. Besides fee-based information, there are free information sources online like Yahoo! Finance, as well as the television stations CNBC, Bloomberg, and FOX Business that give daily news and updates on many companies. My two favorite anchors on CNBC's *Squawk Box* are Becky Quick and Joe Kernen. Suave Kernen asks the hard questions, while Becky's smoothness keeps the show out of trouble. Analysts are frequent guests on many of the TV stations. A good call was made by bank analyst Meredith Whitney on CNBC when she correctly called the subprime mortgage crisis. Brenda Butner hosts an invigorating investing segment on Fox, while on CNBC's *Mad Money*, Jim Cramer uses his extensive knowledge to educate the home gamer. Cramer, an extremely energetic performer, goes out of his way to make investing fun. If you watched his show in the early days, you may have been turned off by his ranting and raving, but his show has come a long way. If you haven't seen it lately, give it a try.

Daily financial news plays a huge part in the decisions of day traders, while long-term investors usually tune out the majority of the news. Long-term investors purchase stocks based on company financials and their perception of the company's future.[72]

Positive news has a tremendous effect on the economy, especially when retail establishments and home builders report excellent earnings with high margins. If retail reports earnings with low margins and builders issue a grim outlook, the markets may be in for some rough sailing. Often, when positive news is lacking, the doldrums invade our psyche, causing spending to slow. When the Iraq invasion occurred in 2003, the markets plummeted and retail shopping practically came to a standstill. Assuming it was a buying opportunity, I purchased many shares of various stocks. The prices continued to decline after my purchase, and instead of waiting for prices to stabilize and rise, I sold my shares. This was not a good strategy, because prices eventually rose after President Bush appeared on television asking everyone to shop. As women responded to his call, shopping till they dropped, the complexion of the markets changed.

Negative news is never beneficial for an economy, but the bearish action negative news generates is necessary to help keep the markets flowing. We can use the news to help us increase our financial position by selling stocks when the news is positive and buying when the news is negative. This is often a difficult concept to grasp. The following hypothetical scenarios indicate how, without either buyers or sellers, the markets would suffer.

If everyone was a buyer, there would be no sellers.

- Hypothetically, if there was only positive news and no sellers, the markets would be fully saturated. No new money would be coming into the market.

If everyone was a seller, there would be no buyers.
- Hypothetically, if there was only negative news, with no one investing in the marketplace, the market value would decline.

This hypothetical scenario is just a supposition. In our marketplace, we can always count on the contrarians who will go against the grain and keep the markets flowing.

Online Trading Pros and Cons

The following information should be helpful for women determined to work online alone. Trading online is the same as entering into any other type of contract. In order for a trade to be executed, there must be someone on the other end of that trade. Stocks can be purchased and held long-term or they can be traded daily.

It may seem like the Internet has always been a part of our life, but actually it is a fairly recent phenomenon. There are various time frames suggesting when the Internet came into existence, starting as early as the sixties and seventies. My husband and I purchased our first IBM computer in the early eighties, and the Internet wasn't available in our area at that time. After our homes were invaded by cyberspace reality, online trading became an option, with trades made through an exchange that matches buy and sell orders. After signing with a broker licensed to trade stocks, you won't have to speak directly to anyone unless assistance is needed. Anyone with a computer, Internet access, and enough moola to open an account can buy and sell at his or her own convenience. Online traders are usually self-motivated and independent and feel they do not need the expertise of a broker. At the onset, trading was dominated by men, but women soon began entering the game. By 2002, women made up 33 percent of online traders.[73]

Online trading firms have competitive pricing, with commissions under $10 per trade. The top-ranked brokers also have a full range of trading tools, from stock screeners to streaming quotes. Fidelity offers before- and after-hours trading.[74]

> **Online trading companies' costs in 2009:**
>
> | | |
> |---|---|
> | Fidelity | $7.95 per trade |
> | E*Trade | $9.99 per trade |
> | TD Ameritrade | $9.99 per trade |
> | Charles Schwab | $8.95 per trade |

Is Day-Trading Right for You?

Have you been hearing a lot of chatter about day-trading? The following questions should help give some direction.

1. When the market has huge gains, what do you do?
    a. Sell *(High tolerance for risk)
    b. Buy (Low tolerance for risk)
2. When everyone is buying, what do you do?
    a. Sell *(High tolerance for risk)
    b. Buy (Low tolerance for risk)
3. When everyone is selling, what do you do?
    a. Sell (Low tolerance for risk)
    b. Buy *(High tolerance for risk)

Answers: * High tolerance for risk = day trader
Low tolerance for risk = long-term investor

The answers to these questions should give you a better understanding of whether or not to avoid day-trading. Women with a high tolerance for risk could do well day-trading, while women with a low tolerance for risk may be better off in safer investment areas.

Day-trading may sound easy and fun, yet it is not one-size-fits-all. A day trader must be a risk taker who not only enjoys a challenge but can afford losses. Loss affordability is the key factor, because there will be many days when losses are the name of the game. Of course, there will be other days when stocks prices will escalate. Like long-term investors, day traders buy low and sell higher, but instead of waiting for days, months, or years to lock in profits, day traders manage risk by selling the stock they purchased the same day.

During slowing economies, day traders are like machines, buying and selling within seconds or minutes. Profits can be made in a slowing market, but it is more difficult than in an accelerating market. Day traders are interested in the volatility and momentum of a stock rather than its actual value, and they love stocks that move within a predictable trading range. They do not enjoy the complications associated with stocks breaking out of the trading range. Daily news can make the difference between a profit and a loss, so some decisions must be made in a matter of minutes or seconds.

Traders using a margin account are required to maintain a balance that permits leverage of approximately four times the account amount. Positions must be closed out by day's end, or interest must be paid on the overnight balance. This high-risk margin use causes traders to exit losing positions to prevent further losses. Because traders exit positions quickly, they can be huge losers especially in an accelerating market when the market dips and then regains its momentum after the sell. Meir Statman's findings indicate more day traders lose money than make money.[75]

Traders can profit as the market rises or when it falls, depending on whether the trader takes a long or short position. Traders who short stocks purchase the stock from the broker and sell the borrowed stock in the hope the price will fall. If the price falls, the trader purchases the stock at a lower price, locking in a profit. If the price rises, the investor usually covers the position and loses money on the transaction. Since most day traders liquidate all positions by the end of the day, they lock in a loss even if they feel the market may reverse the following day.

Day traders are not easily fooled by how markets open. In a recovering market, markets are more predictable, but in a slowing market many things can happen during the course of a day, causing all sorts of problems. A market may open high and continue up all day, only to reverse at day's end. In a slowing economy, the last hour of trading may give some indication of where the market is headed.

It is never wise to make a lump-sum purchase, and day traders often make this mistake. If markets are on an upward trend, lump-sum purchasing can work well, but in a slowing economy, it is advisable to never purchase more than a fourth of the position you wish to hold. If the market moves down after a purchase, the trader will be happy the entire position was not acquired, and if the price moves up, the best strategy is to let it go rather than chase the stock. It is not necessary to own the entire position.

Although long-term investors smack their lips when markets plunge, day traders find those times very challenging. Of course, long-term investors do not find all market plunges exciting. For example, when the tech market plunged in 2001, value investors were not buying. Value investors would never make the mistake speculators made of buying stocks on the hope of future profitability. Warren Buffett never bought any tech stocks, and he often said he didn't buy anything he didn't understand. Since he is an astute investor, he probably had a difficult time understanding why folks were buying stocks without earnings. Investor profits are generally safer than day-trader profits because long-term investors purchase stocks at lower prices, whereas day traders purchase stocks daily, so base prices are much higher. When the market dives, long-term investors can sell and not lose much of their investment, while day-trader losses are huge. Profits and losses can be made or lost in a thriving economy or in a poor economic setting. The long-term investor does not have the volatile markets with which to contend, so the investment is a little more secure, providing the investment was made after a market decline.

There will always be winners and losers in any market. Day traders generally sell their losers and move on. Professionals are also very quick to sell their losers, yet small investors often prefer to hang on to their stocks for fear they will miss out on any future upside moves—the "fear of future regret" phenomenon. My personal experiences indicate that cut-and-run is the way to go. Behavior analysts have found investors would rather compound errors than admit a mistake was made. Since it is not always possible to pick the right stocks, we should admit we made a mistake and move on.

Although selling losers is the general rule, there are times when riding out losses is preferable. Determining when to do this is difficult. Riding out a loss may be less risky if the loss appears to be temporary and not a problem that can come back to haunt us, as if

- a recession is not on the horizon;
- our stock is best-of-breed;
- the company's fundamentals have not changed;
- the company is not restructuring; or
- the company is not part of a government investigation.

In the seventies, John Meriwether and his bosses at Salomon rode out losses when they found themselves in dire financial trouble over an unanticipated investment reaction. Meriwether understood the art of trading US Treasury-bill futures when many others did not. When J. F. Eckstein and Company was on the verge of failing because of massive margin calls, Meriwether recommended Salomon buy out Eckstein's future securities contracts. Treasury-bill futures generally trade at a discount to the actual T-bills, but in June 1979, this pattern reversed, and futures became more expensive than the actual T-bills. Instead of converging as expected, the gap continued to get wider, and margin calls were made. Meriwether understood prices would converge at some point, and he talked his bosses into taking over the securities.

After they took over the securities, the prices did not converge as Meriwether predicted. Instead of converging, the spread widened over the next few weeks, and it looked like Armageddon for Salomon since a lot of money was tied up in the securities. Even though the losses were mounting, the firm stayed in the game. Finally prices converged just as Meriwether had predicated, and Salomon made an enormous profit. Meriwether was promoted to partner.[76]

Speculative Stock Picking

Although spec stocks are fun to own, they should only be purchased if losing most or all of your investment is not a concern. As a rule, speculative stocks do not perform well, so it is best to stay away from them. That being said, many investors enjoy investing in spec stocks because the risk/reward is usually quite high. I couldn't resist purchasing some speculative stocks from time to time. A few of my picks were winners, but most were losers.

In the eighties, I purchased Telex, a speculative $2 communication stock. At first it looked like dead meat, but after a few years, it began to climb. After it quadrupled in price, I sold it and numbly watched it climb to over $75 per share.

Jim Hackett had a similar experience in the late seventies when he thought cable and satellite TV looked like an interesting investment vehicle. He had been doing research on this innovative investment for a client, and after some thought, he decided to invest in Viacom, one of the companies he thought was best-suited to his investment style. During the first few years he owned the stock, the price barely moved. Feeling as though something must be amiss, Hackett made the decision to sell all his shares. Shortly after he sold, the stock price started to climb and climb.[77]

Even though Telex and Viacom became huge winners, most speculative stocks do not achieve these types of results. An example of a spec stock I own that has not performed well is Trimedyne. In the eighties, a few of my friends and I purchased shares of this speculative surgical-laser company for $5 a share. When the stock price reached over $13 a share, my friends sold their shares, immediately locking in a profit. I did not follow their lead. Instead, I kept my shares, and as the price declined, I bought additional shares. By the early nineties, the share price had dropped to $2. Currently, this company's stock is priced below $1 a share.

Apparently my friends were investment savvy while I, not so much. My stock is now worth only a few cents a share. I still have the certificate, which is probably worth more than the stock.

Another spec stock I purchased was eToys, an Internet retail toy company. In 1997, the eToys IPO was priced at $20 a share, and on the first day of trading, the share price jumped to $76. Anyone who bought shares at the IPO price of $20 and sold into the highs made an enormous profit.

I wish I could say I was in on the IPO. I bought my shares later.

Although eToys appeared to be a winner, shopping online was not yet popular, so it was a huge mistake to make a lump-sum purchase as the stock price began to fall. In June 2000, eToys raised $100,000 million from some wealthy investors known as PIPE or Private Investment in Public Entities. Often after private investors get involved, the stock price plunges. Stocks generally will drop as financing is taking place and then drop again afterward. Private investors prefer stock prices to fall so their investment yields more stock. According to Tom Taulli, private investors are often smarter than company CEOs, so it may be prudent to be cautious when private investors get involved.[78] In March 2001, eToys declared bankruptcy, and I lost my entire investment.

Day-Trading Stock Picks

Although many day traders trade individual stocks, some have turned to trading long and short ETFs. When the economy is slowing, traders often resort to trading short ETFs, while at other times the long ETFs are popular.

Long ETFs tripling an index are extremely volatile, and if traders are on the right side of the trade, huge gains are possible. Since profits can be larger, losses will also be larger. The following long ETFs triple the index.

- **Direxion Small Cap Bull 3X Shares (TNA).** This is a non-diversified fund investing in the performance of the Russell 2000 index.
- **Direxion Daily Emerging Markets Bull 3X Shares (EDC).** This is a non-diversified fund investing in emerging markets.
- **Direxion Daily Energy Bull 3X Shares (ERX).** This non-diversified fund invests in domestic companies in the energy sector.
- **ProShares UltraPro Russell 2000 3X Shares (URTY).** This fund invests in securities and derivatives.

ProShares Hedge Replication ETF (HDG) trade like stocks. Some day traders choose to trade this extremely risky ETF launched on July 14, 2011, as an alternative to hedge funds. It seeks to provide the risk/return characteristic of a broad universe of hedge funds without many of the challenges, such as illiquidity, limited transparency, and high fees. It opened at $40.16 and closed at $40.07 on the first trading day. On Sept 12, 2011, the close was $37.97 and the close on December 21, 2012, was $39.87.[79]

Short ETFs were popular with day traders during the recession, but since the lows in 2009, they have not been doing well, as would be expected. In April 2013, many of these short ETFs will do reverse splits to make it appear as though they are performing better than they actually are. ETFs like these move up when the market is declining. By trading these short-positions, traders hope to offset losses they may incur from going long on other stocks. In hindsight, traders hoping to offset some of their losses selling short have often incurred additional losses as markets made unexpected upward moves. The following are examples of several inverse-equity ETFs.

- **ProShares UltraShort S&P 500 (SDS).** The price fell to $18.13 on January 10, 2012, from a high of $39.12 on July 1, 2010. The closing price was $16.22 on July 12, 2012. A reverse split of one for four was issued on October 5, 2012.

- **ProShares UltraShort Real Estate (SRS).** The fifty-two-week high was $32.68 on May 25, 2010. The fifty-two-week low was $13.75 on April 28, 2011. There was a one for three split on October 13, 2011.
- **ProShares UltraShort Russell 2000 (SJH).** This non-diversified fund invests in derivatives that should have similar returns as twice the inverse of the Russell 2000 index. The fifty-two-week high on August 24, 2010, was $96.84. On July 12, 2012, the close was $34.35. A reverse split on February 25, 2011, was one for four.
- **Direxion Financial Bear 3X Shares (FAZ).** This ETF is extremely risky because it is three times the Russell 1000, which creates short positions by investing over 75 percent of its net assets in financial instruments. As of October 5, 2011, the fifty-two-week high was $81.50. The close on July 12, 2012, was $23.77.

Chart Reading

Reading charts can be helpful if we are careful to actually read the charts and not try to read something into them that isn't there. Two popular charts are the baseline and the head-and-shoulders charts. Anyone interested in additional information on chart reading will find *The Street.com Guide to Smart Investing in the Internet Era* by Dave Kansas an excellent resource.

- A baseline chart is formed after a stock moves up and down for a period of time between what is referred to as *support* and *resistance*. The stock will either move up or down from this base. If the stock appears to be in an upward trend, higher lows will be seen. The next move is through the resistance, with an increase in volume. Volume is important, since it signals interest in the stock. Even if the stock continues up, it may still go down to retest the breakout level. If the stock has support at this resistance level, the stock may be considered a buy.[80]
- The head-and-shoulders chart suggests that a stock is changing course. As with the baseline chart, high volume is important.[81]

Takeaway

- There are many differences between a long-term investor and a day trader.
- Long-term investors invest in the future of a company while day traders look for volatile stocks. Company value is not important to a day trader.
- Long-term investors look forward to huge market plunges while day traders shudder when markets dive.
- Economic news keeps the markets moving, and contrary to popular belief, long-term investors can benefit by keeping abreast of government reports.
- Day trading is not for everyone. Not only risky and challenging, profits can be gained or lost in minutes.
- Margin accounts should be avoided.
- A breakout is when a stock price moves up or down from the range where it had been trading. It is assumed the stock will proceed for some time in the continued direction from where it broke out. Of course, we all know we can never assume.
- A trading range is the style of trading between a certain price range, rising from a support price and falling off a resistance price. Each time the stock hits the high, it falls back to the low, and vice versa. Day traders can either buy the stock at the lower price and sell it as it reaches the resistance price or sell short as it reaches a high, and then buy it back as it reaches its low or support price. A problem often occurs when the stock breaks out of its trading range.
- Premarket trading should be avoided, yet premarket orders are often used by day traders if markets are expected to open up. If the market is on track to open down, traders may purchase stocks soon after the opening. If the market opens up, they may wait to purchase stock until the time of day when the market generally declines. In any case, as soon as the stock price makes an acceptable move, the day trader will sell. This can be done in seconds, minutes, or hours, depending on the stock and what move is acceptable.
- Trend following is when a trader makes trades on the expectation the stock will continue to move higher steadily or decline steadily

for a certain period of time. We know trends can change quickly, so we must always be alert.
- Volatile stocks are very popular with day traders. Some day traders stick with a few volatile stocks that trade on heavy volume, while others look at daily stock news and trade those stocks. In any case, these traders attempt to purchase stock at day lows, and after an acceptable upside move, they sell.

A return of approximately 0 percent is nothing to get excited about, except in the midst of a stock market crash.[82]
—William P. Barrett

7

Cash Is King

"Saving is preserving the value of money not spent." [83]

Saving a percentage of our income should be our number one priority, because our future is never certain. As we have seen, cash was king during recessions and the Great Depression, but maintaining liquid cash in our portfolios is a double-edged sword. If we do not have cash available, we cannot take advantage of investment opportunities; but if we keep too much cash in our portfolios, we will probably fall behind as inflation eats our cash reserve. This is a difficult problem to resolve.

Young people have excellent taste and want nice things. Immediately after graduating and finding a job, they set out to make retailers rich. I can't say I blame them for not wanting to wait, but I was taught anything worth having is worth waiting for. I imagine there will be many who will disagree with me, but nonetheless, that is what I was taught. The other thing I was taught was that no matter how much or how little we earn, we should save at least a small percentage of our income.

I began learning to handle a small allowance when I was young. There are many ways to divide income, and Suze Orman has some excellent ideas on the subject. As a child, I divided my allowance into thirds. The first third went into savings, the second third went into a necessity fund, and the last third was my discretionary fund. I could use the discretionary fund for whatever I chose. I remember a time when I wanted to go somewhere with my friends that was going to deplete my entire cash reserve, so I chose not to go. My friends went, and I remember feeling sad.

I can't remember any specifics about where they went, so obviously it must not have been important.

Having some cash in our portfolio is usually an asset in a slowing economy, but in times of inflation, keeping too much cash usually is not wise. When interest rates are high, taking advantage of compounding can be an excellent savings vehicle, but in times when interest rates are low, our savings most likely will be unable to keep up with inflation, and we could outlive our savings. With the debate in Congress over Social Security programs and the sluggishness of the economy, retirement planning is more important now than ever.

Finding an excellent financial planner and carefully considering his or her advice can put you on a better path to the future. Remember, the advice from a financial planner is a just a recommendation, and it is your responsibility to do your homework on any advice you get. There are many things you can do to help yourself in your golden years, and financial planners are usually on the cutting edge of recommending what works best. Some suggest anyone retiring on a tight budget should consider relocating to a less costly area. Moving can have an enormous impact on quality of life, particularly for those who have significant equity in their homes with little savings elsewhere.[84]

Not planning realistically for retirement can be a huge mistake. Some money managers recommend having access to 70 percent of your preretirement income in order to fund your golden-years lifestyle. Depending on that lifestyle and whether or not your home and automobile are paid off, this may seem high—but factoring in the rise of future health care costs, utilities, gasoline, and insurance, it may be closer than you think.[85] In general, women living alone believe they can live on less than men living alone and I must admit, I believe it is a reasonable assumption. Women have the inclination and the will to live frugally, whereas men may not be able to give up their toys.

In 1979, William E. Simon, secretary of the Treasury, wrote, "The real problem with the dollar is that we're printing too many of them. When you produce too much of anything, the price goes down. No one wants to hold a dollar that's being debased by its own government."[86]

Sound familiar?

One popular vehicle for compounding cash is the certificate of deposit. Unlike money-market funds, CDs are insured by the FDIC up to $250,000 per person per bank. Certain restrictions apply, so it is important to speak with your bank representative. When you purchase a CD, you agree to let the bank keep your money for a specific period of time; if you want to withdraw the money sooner than the expiration, the bank generally imposes a substantial fee. I remember in the eighties, interest rates were climbing, and many folks paid the penalty for early withdrawal in order to purchase another CD with a higher interest rate. They seemed to think it was cost-effective.

Often, we make excuses for not paying ourselves first. Everyone has priorities. Instead of treating yourself to a coffee or a dessert, put that money in a savings vehicle. Living within your means is the key to being sucessful.

> *The problem may not be our income, but what we spend.*

Takeaway

- Living beyond your means is not productive.
- Compounding is when interest is added to the principal.
- The Federal Deposit Insurance Corporation (FDIC) insures passbook savings and CDs up to $250,000 per person per bank with certain conditions applying, so it is best to check with the bank before investing.
- Financial planners usually can help you plan realistically for retirement.

Gold is forever. It is beautiful, useful and never wears out. Small wonder it has been prized over all else.[87]

—*James Blakely*

8

Gold Magic

Folks have enjoyed the beauty and magic of gold since the times of the ancient Egyptians, Greeks, and Romans. It served as a way to preserve wealth and as a hedge against inflation. As the dollar depreciates, gold demand generally rises. Because of its stability and high intrinsic value, gold also rises during times of economic and political uncertainty. There are many ways to own gold, from companies that manufacture it to the actual jewelry, coins, and bullion. Many advisors recommend owning some gold even though, contrary to popular belief, gold stocks are not always winners.

A 2005 study by McClellan Financial Publications shows the correlation between inflation and gold. As inflation rises in times of economic instability, gold prices may be at lower levels. According to the study, inflation has a fourteen-month lag to gold. This appears to be an indicator we should consider as we move forward.[88]

China took over as the world's largest gold producer in 2007. Since gold is an extremely popular commodity with the Chinese, it makes sense that it would be advantageous for China to be a huge gold producer. Despite being the world's main gold producer, China is not exporting any of the bullion it produces.

There is a seasonal demand for gold each year in India during the Hindu religious holidays, festivals, and weddings. Gold is their measure of success, and women love to wear a lot of it. During the mid-March lows, purchases are made, promoting a rally that goes through May. Then a low period occurs from June to late July. Farmers wait for the September monsoons to be over, to see how their crops fare, before they purchase gold. These trends tend to prevail even in secular bear markets.

Gold-Producing Companies

The following companies are among the largest global gold producers.

- **Barrick Gold Corporation (ABX)** is located in North America, South America, and the Australia Pacific region. The closing price on June 23, 2011, was $43.99. The closing price on October 20, 2011, was $44.33, and on December 21, 2012, the close was $33.38.[89]
- **Newmont Mining Corporation (NEM)** is a holding company that mines in the United States, Australia, Peru, Indonesia, Ghana, Mexico, and New Zealand. NEM engages in acquisition exploration and the production of gold and copper. The closing

price on June 23, 2011, was $53.98. The closing price on October 20, 2011, was $61.64, and the close on December 21, 2012, was $44.58.[90]
- **AngloGold Ashanti (AU)** primarily engages in the exploration and production of gold. AU also produces silver, uranium oxide, and sulfuric acid. The company conducts gold-mining operations in South Africa and continental Africa, including Ghana. The closing price on June 23, 2011, was $42.46. The closing price on October 20, 2011, was $39.67, and the close on December 21, 2012, was $30.34.[91]
- **DRDGOLD Limited (DRD)**, an ADR gold miner in South Africa, is one of the world's top gold producers, along with China and India. The closing price of DRD on June 23, 2011, was $4.35. The closing price on October 20, 2011, was $5.54, and the close on December 21, 2012, was $7.25.[92]
- **Goldcorp, Inc. (GG)**, a gold-mining company based in Canada, has the lowest cash costs of any tier-one mining company and produces 2.3 million ounces. The closing price of GG on June 23, 2011, was $48.65. The closing price on October 20, 2011, was $44.57, and the close on December 21, 2012, was $35.20.[93]

Gold Mutual Funds and Gold Commodity Funds

Some gold mutual funds and gold commodity funds are backed by physical gold, while others are not. Gold mutual funds and gold stocks are not always winners, although recently it appeared as though most gold funds were making money. Gold Bullion Security Funds are mandated to keep the bulk of their net assets in precious metals with a small percentage in cash.

- **The Central Fund of Canada, Ltd. (CEF)** holds mostly gold and silver. The CEF is a closed-end fund that trades on the NYSE and is headquartered in Canada.[94]
- **The Central Gold Trust Common (GTU)** holds primarily gold bullion in both bar and certificate form. The GTU is a closed-end fund trading on the NYSE and is headquartered in Canada.[95]

The Rise and Fall of Gold

Gold not only has intrinsic value, it is generally considered a safe haven in both bull and bear markets. Just as the value of gold skyrocketed recently, it made a similar move in the eighties before the Central Bank began dumping it. After the free fall, I purchased a gold mutual fund. I believed gold prices would rebound, and wanting to take advantage of the upside move I assumed was coming, I made a onetime large lump-sum purchase.

Fully vested and ready for my investment to grow, I waited.

My assumption proved wrong. Instead of gold prices rising, they continued to decline, and my fund lost much of its value. After watching my investment dwindle, I sold all my shares, locking in a huge loss.

Not only did I commit the mistake of lump-sum purchasing, I committed a second mistake of selling into the lows.

Prices did not move much after that time until 2004, when gold prices began slowly trending upward again. In early 2013, some professionals still continue to recommend gold as an investment. They may be correct in their thinking, but my past experience with gold has left me skeptical.

Exchange-Traded Gold Funds

One of the main differences between iShares and SPDR Gold Trust (GLD) is that iShares create roughly a hundred shares from every ounce of gold, whereas GLD creates roughly ten shares per ounce. iShares are more accessible for day traders playing the gold market.[96]

- **iShares Gold Trust (IAU)** represents a cost-efficient alternative to investments in physical gold for investors not otherwise in a position to participate directly in the market. Price, net asset value, and holding amounts of gold are available daily. Vault inspections are conducted twice a year, and inspection certificates are available. IAU is not an investment company. It receives gold deposits in exchange for the creation of baskets of iShares and sells gold to cover trust liabilities. The IAU launched in January 2005 and is listed on the New York and Toronto stock exchanges. The trust owned over fifty-four tonnes of gold in November 2007 and

was backed by physical gold held in vaults in New York, Toronto, and London. As of July 29, 2010, the fund claimed to hold 90.88 tonnes of gold in storage. On the negative side, some investors doubt iShares has sufficient gold inventory to back existing warehouse receipts. The IAU share price was $16.92 on August 4, 2011, and $15.62 on March 20, 2013.[97]
- **SPDR Gold Trust (GLD)** is listed on the NYSE and owns 82,000 gold bars weighing 400 troy ounces each. Some $31 billion in bullion is stashed away in an HSBC vault in London, where it is audited twice a year. The GLD has an extremely complex prospectus and may have a conflict of interest in its relation with HSBC and JPMorgan Chase, which are believed to have large short-positions in gold. Some gold buyers don't trust this fund or any other investment they can't hold in their hands.

In 1933, Franklin Roosevelt ordered Americans to sell privately held gold to the government, and the Federal Reserve paid $20.67 per ounce. Some privately held gold escaped this sale, and a year later, when the dollar was devalued, gold sold for $35 an ounce. Anyone still owning some coins turned a nice profit.[98] When investors purchase coins and bars from dealers, a 5 percent to 10 percent markup is added to the spot price, and when selling coins, another 5 percent or more is added to the selling price.[99]

Gold Krugerrand Coins

Krugerrands are an international symbol of wealth and prestige. First released in 1967, they are the world's first modern bullion gold coin and remain one of the most popular gold coins ever minted.

The South African Krugerrand sells for a 4.5 percent premium to the value of the gold in it. There is a markup when you buy it and then a markdown of about 5 percent when you sell it. In the past, a one-ounce Krugerrand coin could have been purchased for approximately $300, while today a single-ounce coin would go for approximately five times that amount.

Gold Jewelry

Gold jewelry has always been popular with women, and it has become the standard for an expression of love. As women and men express their love, they adorn their fingers with this beautiful metal. One of my best friends, Doris Wong, loved gold, and she purchased many pieces of twenty-two-carat gold jewelry because she remembered how it had been a valuable asset for her family on their way to America from China. Although she passed away, her children have inherited some magnificent, valuable jewelry.

Gold prices are often directly related to India's buyers, who purchase a lot of gold during the wedding and festival seasons each year. Like Doris, they love jewelry, and since it is a status symbol, they wear as many pieces as possible at one time.

In 2011, gold home parties became popular in some parts of the United States. Gold buyers were invited to attend the parties. Buyers weighed the gold owners were willing to sell and made offers. I never attended any of these parties but I have been told gold owners received what they felt was a fair price for their gold.

Jewelers

Jewelers can be divided into high-end, medium, and low-end. Tiffany and Finlay Enterprises are high-end jewelers. They generally benefit from rising gold prices, because as gold prices rise, gold jewelry becomes more valuable. Demand for gold jewelry was up 22 percent in 2007. Shares in Tiffany (TIF) closed at $69.14 on August 4, 2011. The closing price on December 21, 2012, was $58.40.[100] The close on April 12, 2013, was $73.67.

Low-end to medium jewelry companies tend to suffer from increasing gold prices, since lower-income-level clientele are less adaptable to price changes. Examples of medium to low-end companies include:

- **Blue Nile Inc. (NILE)** closed at $30.44 on August 19, 2011. The close on April 12, 2013, was $32.21.[101]
- **Signet Jewelers (SIG)** closed at $32.09 on August 10, 2011. The close on April 12, 2013, was $68.[102]
- **Zale Corporation (ZLC)** closed at $2.26 on October 3, 2011. On April 12, 2013, the close was $4.22.[103]

Takeaway

- In 2007, China took over as the world's largest gold producer. Since gold is an extremely popular commodity with the Chinese, it makes sense that it would be advantageous for China to be a huge gold producer.
- There are many kinds of gold mutual funds and gold commodity funds. Some are backed by physical gold and some are not.
- Gold is considered to be a good investment, but there are times when the price of gold may fall. Holding gold for the long term has proven to be lucrative.
- Tiffany and Finlay Enterprises are high-end jewelers. Signet Groups, Zale, and Blue Nile are low-end to medium jewelry companies.
- Since gold is a status symbol in India, women love to wear as many pieces of jewelry as possible at the same time. Gold prices have been directly related to the timetable of India's buyers, who buy during the wedding and festival seasons each year.
- The gold Krugerrand, introduced in 1967, was the first modern bullion gold coin. It remains one of the most popular gold coins ever minted.
- When inflation rises in times of economic instability, we may see gold prices at lower levels.
- One of the main differences between iShares and SPDR Gold Trust (GLD) is iShares creates roughly a hundred shares from every ounce of gold, whereas GLD creates roughly ten shares per ounce. This makes iShares more accessible for day traders or small investors wishing to play the gold market.

People expect that trends that existed in the recent past will continue in the future.[104]

—*Meir Statman*

9

Red Flags

Bankruptcy Surprises

Hearing the word "bankruptcy" often puts fear in those who are involved with a company filing for protection. Employees of companies filing for bankruptcy fear they will lose their jobs, and clients fear companies will not honor their contracts. Stockholders fear loss of net worth, and creditors as well as bond holders (who actually are creditors) fear loss of their investments. There are special rules for various types of bankruptcies or reorganizations, but in general there is a hierarchy of creditors, starting with the liquidators, the government taxes, and the first bondholders.

Company reorganization usually indicates a problem and it should trigger a "sell" for investors. If a best-of-breed company reports a disappointing quarter, small investors may purchase the stock because of the lower stock price, while professionals will avoid that stock. If a company has more than one disappointing quarter, the rule should be to stay away from that stock; if a company whose stock you own appears to be headed into bankruptcy, you should run, not walk, away from the stock. Professionals will cut and run when a company issues its first disappointing financial report. Nothing good ever comes from holding a company stock as it moves lower and files for bankruptcy protection.

Bankruptcy laws actually protect failing businesses by allowing a methodical way to liquidate or reorganize while compensating creditors. Most cases are filed under Chapter 7, 11, or 13 in federal court, since bankruptcy cases cannot be filed in a state court. Bankruptcy filing usually occurs when a company's debt is larger than its ability to pay off creditors. Older established businesses are less likely to enter bankruptcy than newly formed companies, but we should always remain cautious. The reality of bankruptcy is that businesses often emerge as more viable companies after they have been purged of most of their debt.

In 2009, when General Motors Company emerged from Chapter 11 reorganization bankruptcy backed by the US government, the UAW collective-bargaining agreement was not torn up, as it would have been in a typical company bankruptcy.[105] GM turned profitable in 2011, and investors are hopeful this mishap will not come back to hurt the company in the future.

Although bondholders are usually the first creditors in line to recover their losses, sometimes they only receive a small portion of their investment. An example of this was how the GM bondholders faired after the company emerged from bankruptcy. In 2003, schoolteacher Debra June invested $70,000, a big chunk of her savings, in GM bonds. She told John Roberts of CNN's *American Morning* that as of June 1, 2009, her $70,000 investment was worth approximately $200.[106] Although the government gave stock and warrants to bondholders to help make up for their losses, many investors are reluctant to put money into other companies having government involvement.

The first stock I owned was Penn Central, a thriving railroad company. Stock prices had been in the $60 price range, so when prices fell to $15 per share, I purchased additional shares. I continued making purchases as prices declined. By the time Penn Central declared bankruptcy, I owned many shares.[107] Around this time in 1970, a young college student named Steve Forbes was looking for a sound investment. Knowing the stock price had declined but not realizing Penn Central was in trouble, Forbes editor James W. Michaels recommended Penn Central. When Penn Central entered bankruptcy, Michaels and other savvy investors were as surprised as I was. Penn Central emerged from bankruptcy as Conrail for freight and Amtrak for passengers, run by the government. Michaels predicted new securities would be issued and suggested investors buy them.[108] Although Forbes profited from the new securities issued, I did not.

Another stock I owned that proceeded into bankruptcy was White Motor, a Cleveland, Ohio, trucking manufacturer that went from producing automobiles, buses, and various sizes of high-quality trucks to producing only large trucks. I purchased this stock as the company was about to merge with White Consolidated Industries. I did not know the merger attempt would be blocked by the government. Although the government later removed the blockage, the merger was never completed. The company went into bankruptcy in 1980, and I lost my entire investment.

Morrison Knudsen, an engineering and construction company where my husband worked, filed for bankruptcy protection in 1995. Since it was the first time most of the employees—including my husband—had ever been involved in a bankruptcy filing, there were many concerns. A few young engineers left the company for other jobs, and a few clients canceled their contracts, but since seasoned employees stayed with the sinking ship, business continued as usual. This company had survived the Great Depression and eighty-three years of various other economies, having built major projects like the Hoover Dam, the San Francisco/Oakland Bay Bridge, and the Trans-Alaska pipeline. As Morrison Knudsen struggled to survive its corporate problems, the stock price fell from $30 per share to $5.75. An optimist, I never suspected the company would enter bankruptcy, so I bought additional shares. When the company filed for bankruptcy protection, the stock price fell to zero, wiping out my entire investment.

This company emerged from bankruptcy with some changes to the benefits package; a new owner, Dennis Washington; and a new name, Washington Group International. The new owner purchased Morrison Knudsen for $380 million and retained current management and dedicated employees. Business continued as usual. Six years later, in 2001, Washington Group International filed for bankruptcy protection, virtually eliminating all shareholder value, and again my entire investment was lost. Most employees were surprised, but in hindsight, it should have been predictable, since many of the older seasoned engineers with the highest salaries had been retired or laid off prior to the filing.[109]

URS Group purchased what remained of Washington Group International in 2007 for $3.1 billion, or $95.11 per share. Having purchased the company six years earlier for $380 million, Dennis Washington walked away a winner. Since URS retained the managerial team from Washington Group International, I have resisted purchasing any of this company stock.

Hopefully, this means I have finally learned.

Although bankruptcy helps debt-ridden companies, shareholders are the losers. Anytime a company is having financial problems, investors should be cautious.

> *There is nothing to be gained by holding stocks on their way to bankruptcy.*

Takeaway

- Company reorganization usually indicates a problem, and it should trigger a "sell" for investors.
- Bankruptcy laws protect troubled businesses, allowing for a systematic way to compensate creditors and help companies reorganize or liquidate. Most cases are filed under Chapter 7, 11, or 13 in federal court, since bankruptcy cases cannot be filed in a state court.
- It is never wise to hold on to a stock if the company is having problems and potentially could file for bankruptcy.
- Bankruptcy helps debt-ridden companies handle debt, but shareholders are the losers.

The future is never clear; you pay a very high price in the stock market for a cheery consensus. Uncertainty actually is the friend of the buyer of long-term values.[110]

—*Warren Buffett*

10

Strategy Review

One of the most important strategies an investor should acquire is diversification. From the time I was a youngster, I was taught never to put all my eggs in one basket, and this concept should apply to anyone investing in the markets. If the game changes, you'll have better chances if you own different types of investments.

> *Putting all your eggs in one basket is not a good strategy.*

Another important strategy investors should use is incremental purchasing. Purchasing a smaller portion of the position allows for error in timing. If the stock goes down after the initial purchase, additional shares can be purchased, effectively dollar-cost averaging. If the price rises after the purchase, the investor is getting the benefit of the higher price. It is not necessary to own the entire position.

A lump-sum purchase is rarely a good plan. In addition to being diversified and purchasing stocks in increments, we should learn when it is advantageous to take profits. Profit-taking at an appropriate stage during a market movement can make the difference between success and failure. Anyone taking a profit prior to a market crash locks in profits while others sustain huge losses. The following strategies are presented for review and quick access in times of indecisiveness.

- Buying at the absolute bottom is certainly an excellent plan, but since it is difficult to predict the exact bottom, a more logical approach is to make a few small purchases as the market appears to be nearing the bottom. Since markets generally make a huge upside move as they burst out from the bottom, owning a few stocks as the market reverses could prove advantageous.
- Although it is often difficult to determine the market trend, sitting on the sidelines usually is not a good strategy.
- Selling into market highs is a good strategy, even if the market continues up after the sell.
- Buying at the top is nearly always a mistake. Missing the upside move is not nearly as bad as buying at the top before a market plummets. Waiting for dips even in a market moving in an upward trend is often advantageous. The market generally will take a breather. Sometimes the pullback is short, while at other times it can be quite substantial.
- It is wise to avoid buying hard-to-understand products. From time to time brokers may recommend various products in order to increase client profits, but make it a rule to never participate.
- There is no free lunch. Since "free" information often comes with an agenda, it's wise to be cautious.
- Be prepared for change in a slowing economy. Whatever is happening, it may change quickly.
- Unsuspecting traders sometimes fall for the takeover game. A stock is hyped based on a takeover rumor, and as the stock price rises, unscrupulous investors liquidate their positions. After liquidation, the takeover is denied and the stock price drops, leaving the trader holding a stock worth much less than when it was purchased just hours before.
- Buying a stock after it moves down and as it begins making a turn up is usually a good strategy. This is usually referred to as the V turn, indicating selling may have ended.
- It's important to check out company financials before purchasing a stock if the stock you are buying is for an investment.

- It is never bad to take a profit, but selling a stock as it is beginning a ramp upward is not a good strategy. Selling as the market becomes saturated is a better strategy. Safety measures should be put into place so gains will not be lost if the trend changes direction prematurely.
- Adding to stock positions if a stock dips for no reason is a good strategy.
- Bankruptcy laws protect troubled businesses and allow for a systematic way to compensate creditors and reorganize. Holding stocks as companies head into bankruptcy is not a good plan.
- It is not wise to buy stock when a top analyst downgrades it, unless the company appears to have been downgraded for reasons other than fundamentals or being under investigation.
- Never buy stocks of cyclical companies in a poor economy; they need a strong economy to do well. Cyclical stocks thrive when an economy is starting to improve. Businesses sensitive to interest rates are cyclical in nature because rates are closely linked to economic performance. Other stocks that do well as economies begin to flourish are retailers, hotels, restaurants, and car manufacturers.
- Buying the stock of a company that is doing secondary financing is never a good idea.
- Allowing company loyalty to rule when making an investment decision is not wise. It is best not to invest in the company where you or your family members work.
- Traders should not buy stock of a company that is part of collateral damage (when one company takes down an entire sector), but it is a great time for investors to buy best-of-breed companies.
- It is never a good idea to purchase the stock of companies doing reverse splits. This is an indication a company is trying to disguise its low value. Some company stocks have improved after a split, but the reward is not worth the risk.
- Holding stock of a company having financial problems is a bad plan. The company could file for bankruptcy. Why take a chance when there are so many other company stocks you can own with less risk?
- It is never wise to chase a stock when it is spiking or when it is in free fall.

- Buying stock when a top analyst upgrades the stock may be a good strategy, although it may not work if the stock has already had a great run.
- Long-term investors should not purchase stocks with high price/earnings ratios. A low P/E indicates the stock is cheap, and a high P/E indicates the stock is overpriced.
- Anytime a company reports disappointing earnings should be a red flag. Often after a company reports a serious decline in earnings, the stock price drops. The best strategy may be to sell as soon as the earnings report is announced. There are times a poor report does not affect the stock price, but why hold on to the stock?
- Buying excellent stocks cheap is good, but buying cheap stocks is bad. Warren Buffett has said we should buy stocks we would be perfectly happy to hold if the market shut down for ten years.[111] He and many other investors have benefited from this buying technique. He has also said he buys stocks that are cheap but not cheap stocks. This is an important distinction.
- Selling higher than the price paid is always a good strategy. All profits are good.

Predictable and Preventable Mistakes

Historically, best-of-breed companies delivered huge profits over the long term. The market never moves in a straight line so the upside moves were generally followed by dips and then moves up. To help with future posturing, this summary of predictable and preventable mistakes will help you make sense of the markets and stay on the successful path.

- Traders should not be fooled when markets close up in a bear market. The days following market crashes often see stock prices move up after the initial plunge. Depending on the severity of market problems, traders may not want to buy stocks when prices begin to fall. Waiting for additional plunges before committing any money to the market is a less risky plan.
- Paying attention to subtle signs of what is happening in the economy can be helpful as we contemplate investing opportunities.

- Being cautious in a poor economy is important, since unforeseen events can add to problems. For example, during the Depression, dust storms prevented farmers from being able to grow food, turning a bad situation into a worse situation.
- The economy will improve before unemployment declines. We should not let high unemployment numbers keep us out of the market if other indicators are good.
- We should cut our losses early when a market begins a free fall, since holding on to stocks as prices plummet can be a painful experience. If we choose, we can repurchase the stock later at a lower price. In the same context, if we do not cut our losses early, we should not sell when the market hits bottom, since it is generally too late to sell at that point. By that time, we should begin looking at bargain prices and add to our positions, effectively dollar-cost averaging.
- Pay attention when stock prices plummet suddenly in the last hour of trading. On October 23, 1929, the day before the market crash, stock prices began plunging, and observant investors cut their losses. Nothing good ever comes from holding on to stocks during market free falls.
- Investing in best-of-breed companies as prices bottom is usually a good choice. A messenger paid $1 a share for White Sewing Machine on October 29, 1929. The stock had been trading at $48 per share a year earlier.
- Keeping some cash in your portfolio for a rainy day is a good strategy. Trying to raise cash during poor economic times is usually a fruitless endeavor.
- Consider refraining from selling at market bottoms. Instead of selling at the lows, purchase best-of-breed stocks for the long term. If we had purchased certain stocks during the market lows from October 2008 to March 2009 and sold them during the April 2011 highs or later, we would have had some outstanding profits.
- Knowing when to buy and when to sell can make the difference between success and failure. Buying on the dips and selling into the advances is the name of the game. Day traders will usually trade the same volatile stocks over and over again.

- Market timing can mean the difference between a profit and a loss. Stocks move up and down daily, so timing is especially crucial for a day trader. Being at the wrong end of a trade during the day can be a disaster. Long-term investors should purchase stock after prices have plummeted, if prices have declined for reasons other than poor fundamentals or being under investigation.
- Commissions should be considered to be part of the cost of trading. If many trades are made daily, online brokers usually charge lower fees. Depending on the number of trades made, costs can be substantial.
- Research makes a huge difference if a quick trading decision is needed.
- Cyclical sectors do well during times of economic prosperity, and holding stocks in these sectors is usually a good plan. Examples of cyclical sector stocks are machinery companies, furniture companies, retailers, hotels, and restaurants. We should remember not to hold these stocks during poor economic times.
- Secular sector stocks usually do well in any economy. As the economy declines, these companies will continue to have growth, since they are recession-proof. Examples of sector stocks are food and manufacturers of personal items. Bonds and T-bills are also considered secular.
- Volatility can create huge profits or huge losses. Day traders use volatility as an opportunity to make enormous profits. If prices plummet without warning, losses can be huge. Profits gained over a few weeks may easily be lost in one day if the wrong stock or the wrong sector is purchased. This can occur in a bull market or a bear market.
- Increased volume in a stock that normally doesn't have a lot of volume may indicate a rumor, support, or interest. A lot of interest in a stock makes it appear less risky to either buy or sell, depending on the trend. Sometimes a rumor is started and the stock soars, only to plummet when the rumor is dismissed.
- Contrary to popular belief, profits and losses can be made in both bull and bear markets. During bull markets, traders may feel it is easier to make profits, but even in a bull market there will be dips that look like the start of another bear market. There are always

winner stocks in any type of market, but often it is difficult to know whether to buy, sell, or hold as the stock price fluctuates.
- It is wise to listen to the media with reservations. Often when news is released, the stock price will either jump or fall before returning to its normal pricing within a short period of time. This should be taken into consideration before taking any action.
- A trader should avoid buying stocks in unpopular sectors, whereas value investors should begin looking for best-of-breed companies in these same sectors. Entire sectors may or may not return to their previous status, and even if the sector returns, some stocks may never make a comeback.
- Straying from the herd is difficult but well worth the effort. Traders should not let the actions of others control their emotions. Safety in numbers is a fallacy. When markets plummet, investors should use those times to search for buying opportunities. Historically, purchases made at market lows have proven to be quite lucrative.
- A trader should make it a rule never to take a large position in a company prior to the release of its financial report. The market reacts in different ways to the news. If the company reports good financials, the stock price may drop because of a prediction of a negative outlook for the following quarter, a downgrade by an analyst, or the fact that the stock price already had a huge upside move. There are other times when the financial report looks ghastly, but the stock price rises because of an upgrade, a better future outlook, or financials that, while bad, were not as bad as anticipated by the street.
- We should never put all our assets into what may appear to be a "sure thing," since nothing is certain.
- Avoiding premarket and after-hours trading is wise. Prices during these times are usually quite different from prices during regular trading hours. Although trading at those times is risky, taking advantage of market differences can sometimes be profitable. A day trader may profit if a stock price plummets in premarket and rises after the market opens—but if the stock declines further after the market opens, the trader may not be a happy camper.
- Making purchases in increments as markets move lower is an excellent strategy. Taking small positions and adding to those positions is safer than lump-sum investing. If the market changes

direction prematurely, there is solace in recognizing the risk was small yet the portion purchased will be moving up. If the market dips again, additional purchases can be made.

- Buying aggressively after a depression or recession appears to be over is usually a mistake. It is nearly always best to purchase stocks in increments, and it is even more important immediately after a depression or recession.
- Taking the good times for granted is usually a mistake.
- Emotions should never enter into an investing decision. If a stock is getting pricey, it is best not to chase it. Waiting for the price to dip is a good strategy—just as when women shop, we wait for a sale. Getting stock at a reasonable price is the name of the game.
- Traders should refrain from buying stocks on the margin, since using leverage to purchase stock is risky. Sometimes a stock will have a huge temporary plunge only to recover the next day or several days later.
- Online trading commissions are lower than traditional full-service firms' commissions but when trying to decide whether to invest with a broker or work alone, commission costs should not be the determining factor.
- Owning a lot of stock in your workplace is usually a mistake. Enron employees learned this lesson the hard way.
- It is never wise to dismiss all rumors concerning a company. It is best to be less trusting of top management in your workplace. Remain cautious even as rumors are denied by top management. The old adage "Where there's smoke, there's fire" may apply.
- Traders need to keep a watchful eye on the market, and it is often difficult to do when traveling. Markets can change quickly, especially in a slowing economy.
- Owning too many stocks or too few stocks at any time can be troublesome.
- Never purchase speculative stocks unless you are willing to risk losing your entire investment. As a rule, most speculative stocks do not perform well. Of course, there are exceptions, but finding them is difficult.
- Never purchase stocks on a whim. A stock being hyped in premarket may reverse and turn negative after the market opens.

Strategy Review

- Don't sell a growth stock too early in the game. Buying a growth stock and selling it before it has time to make ample gains is not a winning plan. Exhibiting patience and discipline is better when investing for the long term.
- Learning from the mistakes of others is preferable to learning from our own mistakes—unless we are using the innovative learning game Kapitall.
- Never repeat your mistakes. This is very difficult, because we are human and mistakes are part of our DNA.
- We can choose to live simply and invest all we can, or we can choose to live from paycheck to paycheck, spending everything we make. The decision is ours.

The difference between playing the stock market and the horses is that one of the horses must win.

—*Joey Adams*

11

Wall Street Lingo

To get a clear understanding of the marketplace, it is essential that you grasp the Wall Street lingo. I've defined some of the terminology you're must likely to encounter and divided the information into sections in an effort to give a clear understanding of how all the various terms are related.

Banks with Economic Power

Central banks have supervisory powers to intercede in times of financial crisis. They have the power to keep banks and other institutions from reckless or fraudulent behavior, and they are usually free from political interference and prosecution.

- **The Federal Reserve Bank (the Fed)** is the US central bank and is headquartered in Washington, DC. It oversees all banks in the United States and regulates the interest rates smaller banks are charged.
- **The European Central Bank (ECB)** is headquartered in Frankfurt, Germany, and is an important central bank for the Euro.

- **The People's Bank of China (PBC)** is a very large central bank that controls monetary policy and regulates financial institutions in mainland China.

Company Performance

- **Buyback** is when a company buys its own shares, usually as a way to stabilize stock prices. An example is Apple computer. As of April 2013, the company has announced a buyback. The stock price has fallen from around $700 to under $400 and it is hoped that the price will increase.
- **Collateral damage** occurs when one company has a setback and takes down all similar companies in the industry.
- **Corporate restructuring** is usually implemented when a company has problems. It should be a concern for investors because it generally indicates financial problems. Sometimes this can be part of a slowing economy, while other times it may be an isolated company problem.
- **Mergers and Acquisitions (M&A)** refers to the combining of companies by acquiring, by being acquired, or by being part of a joint venture.
- **Price/Earnings Ratio (P/E)** is the measure of corporation performance. A higher P/E equals a riskier stock.
- **Revenues** are the amount of money a corporation receives from the sales of its services or products.
- **Reverse splits** are done for various reasons. Since a high stock price often gives the appearance of being more secure, a reverse split may be used to give this illusion. If the price falls below $5, certain institutions may be prohibited from owning the stock. Many advisors warn that these stocks should be avoided.

Contracts

- **Calls or call options** give an investor the right but not the obligation to purchase a stock within a certain time period at an agreed upon price. Investors who buy calls are bullish.

- **Puts or put options** are contracts used to protect profits. They are a bet against a stock. Puts become more valuable as stock prices go down and are often used instead of taking a short position.

Dollar-Cost Averaging

When investors dollar-cost average, they purchase additional shares of stock they already own as prices drop, generating a lower base price.

Indication of the Economy

Since the economy is complex, the markets may be moving in one direction and suddenly change course. Looking at the past can help with determining the future. It has been noted that markets often move approximately six months ahead of economic reports. In other words, the economy usually lags behind the market.

As you attempt to determine the fate of the stock market, bear in mind that short-term market movements are never reliable. Long-term markets will likely continue to move upward, but in order for your portfolio to prosper, you must purchase winning stocks at low prices.

The National Bureau of Economic Research (NBER) provides start and end dates for US recessions. The economy may improve before NBER officially announces the improvement. Market indicators usually refer to government reports, but personal observations can be useful as well. These are some of the most popular government reports:

- **Consumer price index (CPI)** measures the cost of living, as in the change in prices of consumer goods and services over time. It can be an indicator of inflation.
- **Durable goods reports** on goods sold indicate how the economy is doing according to whether or not the consumer is purchasing items, such as cars, refrigerators, TVs, and others items that are not purchased often.
- **Gross domestic product (GDP)** is the official recognized market value of all goods and services produced within a country during a specific period of time.

- **Producer price index (PPI)** measures the average change in selling prices producers receive for their goods.

Investors

- **Contrarian investors** do the opposite of what others are doing. If everyone is buying, the contrarian sells; if everyone is selling, the contrarian will be looking for bargains to buy.
- **Long-term investors** purchase growth or value stocks and hold them for long periods.
- **Short-term investors** hold stocks for short periods of time.
- **Value investors** are long-term investors who purchase growth or income stocks and hold them for the long term.
- **Short-sellers** bet the market will decline. When the market goes against their bets, a short squeeze occurs, meaning the stock price rises quickly and short-sellers want out. As short-sellers cover their positions, mass buying sends prices higher.

Margin Buying or Leverage Buying

Some traders use this method of buying stocks by borrowing funds from the broker and paying a fee, similar to borrowing funds from a banker to purchase a home. Brokers charge a fee to lend. The stocks must be bought and sold in the same day or additional fees will apply.

Margin calls are made by firms when the stock does not perform as expected. The investor can choose to meet the call by adding more money. If the investor does not meet the call, the stock will be sold by the broker.

Markets

- **Bear market** refers to a poor market continually trending lower, with gloomy outlook projections for the economy.
- **Bull market** refers to an upward trend of the market and occurs when the economy is booming.

- **Initial Public Offering (IPO)** is when a privately owned company goes public. At the time of the offering, an investor can purchase shares of the company that had not been available prior to the offering. If the price goes beyond the price when issued, it is considered a hot deal.
- **Primary market (NIM or New Issue Market)** is where shares of a company are initially offered and sold by a lead underwriter or brokerage firm at a designated price.
- **Secondary market or open market** is where most investors, traders, and companies purchase stock. The NYSE, the NASDAQ, and Over-the-Counter are examples of the Secondary Market.
- **SecondMarket,** opened in April 2009, is a private company stock market for stocks of private companies.

Orders

The following orders may be enacted by traders or investors to buy, sell, or protect against a stock price movement.

- **"Good till cancelled" order (GTC)** is an order placed in advance of a stock reaching that price.
- **Limit orders** are placed to buy or sell shares of a stock at a specific price. If that price is not reached, the order will automatically cancel.
- **Market order** is an order placed to buy or sell shares of a stock at the rate at the time the order is received. This is hardly ever a good method of making a purchase.
- **Stop-loss order** is used as a protective mechanism to keep from losing more than a predetermined amount of money.
- **Stop sell-limit order** is an order stating the exact price at which an investor is willing to sell a stock. If the price is not attainable, the stock will not sell.
- **Program trading** refers to electronically executed trades without any human intervention. These are usually large-scale orders based on predetermined conditions.
- **Profit-taking** is when investors take some money off the table. It has nothing to do with the fundamentals of the company. This

often occurs when markets move higher and investors decide to take out some cash.

Rates of Interest

- **Federal funds rate** is the interest rate one bank charges another bank. The Federal Reserve Bank regulates this rate.
- **London Interbank Offered Rate (LIBOR)** is the short-term interest rate set daily by banks. The rate indicates what the world's preferred borrowers must pay to borrow money. Less preferred borrowers can borrow using the LIBOR rate plus points.
- **Prime rate** is the interest rate banks charge their top corporations and businesses. The prime rate plus a few percentage points are given to less significant customers and individuals.

Securities Investor Protection Corporation (SIPC)

The SIPC is a nonprofit membership corporation that insures cash and securities in customer accounts up to $500,000 in securities and $100,000 in cash in case of bankruptcy. The broker must belong to NASD in order to be covered by the SIPC. Some brokerage firms may have other insurance.

Stocks

- **Best-of-breed stocks** are excellent companies that perform well even during difficult times. Value investors generally purchase these stocks.
- **Common stock** is the everyday class of stock that investors purchase.
- **Convertible preferred stock** shares can be converted or changed into common stock.
- **Cyclical stocks** are closely linked to economic performance and perform well periodically when an economy is starting to do well. Businesses sensitive to interest rates are cyclical in nature.

- **Growth stocks** are stocks of businesses that grow by reinvesting their profits into making improvements and hiring new people.
- **Income stocks** are stocks of businesses that share their profits with their stockholders by issuing a dividend.
- **Preferred stock and common stock** ownership represents partial ownership in a company. The preferred stock owners generally have a larger, more stable dividend, and there is a legal right to claims on the company's earnings if the company defaults. Common stock ownership does not include these rights.
- **Secular stocks** refer to stocks of companies whose growth remains consistent regardless of the economy. Typically, secular stocks are manufacturers of food and drugs.

Stock Market Indexes

The following indexes are indicators measuring change in the value of a representative group of stocks:

- **The Dow Jones Industrial Average** is the most popular and familiar index that we hear quoted daily. It is made up of thirty large-cap blue-chip stocks representing different areas of interest. Although it is an indicator of the overall stock market, it is a bit misleading, since only those thirty companies are tracked, and it is price weighted, meaning the highest priced security in the index exerts a disproportionate influence on the Dow's performance.
- **Dow Jones Composite Average** is made up of the average of the Dow Jones Industrial Average, the Dow Jones Transportation Average, and the Dow Jones Utility Average.
- **S&P 500** measures approximately five hundred leading US public companies based on their trustworthiness, sector representation, and liquidity. It was launched as an index in 1957, and since it is market weighted, many investors believe this index gives a more accurate picture of the general performance of the market.
- **Russell 2000 Index** measures 2,000 of the smallest stocks of the Russell 3000 index. It is an unbiased measure of small-cap performance based on their market cap and index membership. It

is completely reconstituted annually to ensure larger stocks do not distort the performance and characteristics of the small caps.[112]
- **Russell 3000** measures 3,000 large-cap US companies that are market weighted, meaning that the largest stocks have more impact on the index than smaller stocks. The comprehensive and unbiased index measures the performance of US companies representing approximately 98 percent of the investable US equity market. It is completely reconstituted annually to ensure new and growing equities.[113]
- **Wilshire 4500** uses the stocks from the Wilshire 5000 index minus 500 of the companies on the S&P 500 Index. Medium and small capitalization managers use the Wilshire 4500 as a performance benchmark.[114]
- **Wilshire 5000** measures the performance of the broadest index of stocks in the US equity market. The index measures the performance of all US equity securities with readily available price data. The Wilshire 5000 is watched by major institutions, including the Federal Reserve board.
- **NASDAQ** is an electronic market that tracks approximately 4,000 mostly technology-oriented market-weighted stocks. The largest stocks have the most impact on the index.

Trading Exchanges

- **The Electronic Exchange (ECN)** permits thousands of buy and sell orders to be matched quickly without human intervention.
- **NASDAQ American Stock Exchange** was the first US stock exchange to trade online.
- **New York Stock Exchange (NYSE)** is located on Wall Street in New York City, and since it has the tightest requirements for companies to become listed, a company must be financially sound in order to be traded on this exchange.
- **Over-the-Counter Exchange (OTC)** is where stocks trade via a dealer network as opposed to a centralized exchange.

Values

- **Market-to-market** is a daily adjustment of securities and futures to reflect actual market value.
- **Market-weighted** is when the largest stocks have more impact on the index level than smaller stocks.
- **Price-weighted** is when the highest-priced securities exert heavy influence on the index.

Women, don't let mistakes weigh you down. Use them as a platform from which to view the future.

Notes

1 John R. Nofsinger, *Investment Blunders of the Rich and Famous* (Upper Saddle River, NJ: Financial Times, Prentice Hall, 2002), 1.
2 "Cramer: Bernanke, Wake Up," CNBC, August 4, 2007, http://video.cnbc.com/gallery/?video=452808336.
3 "The Beginnings of the New York Stock Exchange," Securities and Investment Data Resource Center, accessed January 28, 2013, http://www.restrictedstockinformation.com/S&I_History_NYSE.html.
4 John Kenneth Galbraith, *The Great Crash 1929* (New York: Houghton Mifflin Harcourt, 2009), 2.
5 Muriel Siebert and Aimee Lee Ball, *Changing the Rules: Adventures of a Wall Street Maverick* (New York: Simon & Schuster, 2002), 4.
6 Women's Financial Network at Siebert, accessed March 11, 2011, http://www.wfn.com/home.asp?pageID=332.
7 Aleksandra Todorova, "The Woman's Guide to Retirement," *SmartMoney*, August 1, 2006, http://www.smartmoney.com/retirement/planning/the-girls-guide-to-retirement-19850/.
8 Elizabeth MacDonald and Chana R. Schoenberger, "The World's Most Powerful Women: The Top 10," *Forbes,* September 17, 2007, 126–130.
9 Luisa Kroll, "World's Richest Self-Made Women," *Forbes*, May 23, 2011, 22.

10 "Oprah Winfrey Interview: America's Beloved Best Friend," Academy of Achievement, February 21, 1991, http://www.achievement.org/autodoc/page/win0int-1.
11 Karen Blumenthal, *Six Days in October: The Stock Market Crash of 1929* (New York: Simon & Schuster, 2002), 47.
12 "Stock market crash," accessed June 19, 2013, http://www.straightdope.com/columns/read/2873/who-made-money-during-the-1929-stock-market-crash.
13 Brian Trumbore, "General Motors," accessed June 19, 2013, http://www.buyandhold.com/bh/en/education/history/2001/generalmotors.html.
14 "Meet the Press transcript for August 1, 2010," *MSNBC*, last updated August 28, 2010, http://www.nbcnews.com/id/38487969/ns/meet_the_press-transcripts#.UalCUZVbzdk.
15 John Rothchild, "When the Shoeshine Boys Talk Stocks," accessed June 19, 2013, *CNNMoney*, http://money.cnn.com/magazines/fortune/fortune_archive/1996/04/15/211503/.
16 Claire Suddath, "Brief History of the Crash of 1929," *Time*, October 29, 2008, http://www.time.com/time/nation/article/0,8599,1854569,00.html.
17 Jennifer Rosenberg, "The Great Depression," *About.com 20th Century History*, accessed April 27, 2011, http://history1900s.about.com/od/1930s/p/greatdepression.htm.
18 Jennifer Rosenberg, "The Great Depression," accessed April 27, 2011, http://history1900s.about.com/od/1930s/p/greatdepression.htm.
19 NBER recession definition, accessed June 22, 2013, http://www.nber.org/cycles/recessions_faq.html.
20 Sharon Boswell and Lorraine McConaghy, "Lights Out Seattle," *Seattle Times*, November 3, 1996, http://community.seattletimes.nwsource.com/archive/?date=19961103&slug=2357609.
21 "Bretton Woods Agreement," InvestorWords.com, accessed April 21, 2011, http://www.investorwords.com/6424/Bretton_Woods_agreement.html.
22 Reshma Kapadia, "Stock Pros Who Survived the Depression," *SmartMoney*, April 15, 2009, http://www.smartmoney.com/invest/stocks/stock-pros-who-survived-the-depression/.
23 "Economists Call It a Recession," *CNN.com*, November 26, 2001, http://money.cnn.com/2001/11/26/economy/recession/.

24 Amy Wallace, "Checkmate at the Yellowstone Club," *New York Times*, June 13, 2009, http://www.nytimes.com/2009/06/14/business/14yellow.html.
25 Bjorgolfur Gudmundsson, accessed June 19, 2013, http://www.huffingtonpost.com/2009/07/31/bjorgolfur-gudmundsson-2n_n_248913.html.
26 "The World's Billionaires: James Packer," *Forbes.com*, www.forbes.com/lists/2008/10billionaires08_james-Packer_KRF_html.
27 Duncan Greenberg and Tatiana Serafin, "Up in Smoke," *Forbes*, March 30, 2009, 78, 80.
28 *The Big Book of Business Quotations: More than 5,000 Indispensable Observations on Commerce, Work, Finance and Management* (Cambridge, MA: Basic Books, 2003), 189.
29 Steve Hamm, "Meir Statman on What Investors Really Want," *Building a Smarter Planet* (blog), September 24, 2010, http://asmarterplanet.com/blog/2010/09/meir-statman-on-what-investors-really-want.html.
30 Warren Buffett interviewed on CNBC, March 20, 2009.
31 Greenberg and Serafin, "Up in Smoke," 76.
32 Meir Statman, "The Mistakes We Make—and Why We Make Them," *Wall Street Journal*, August 24, 2009, http://online.wsj.com/article/SB10001424052970204313604574326223160094150.html.
33 Phil Pearlman interviewed on *Street Signs*, CNBC, August 24, 2011, http://philpearlman.com/2011/08/24/talking-gold-on-cnbc-today/.
34 Roger Lowenstein, "Unconventional Wisdom," *SmartMoney*, August 2006, 48.
35 Dyan Machan, "The World's Greatest Investors," *SmartMoney*, August 2006, 66.
36 Dyan Machan, "Investing with Mr. Irrational," *SmartMoney*, June 2011, 65.
37 Floyd Norris, "David Dreman, Contrarian Fund Manager, Exits Unbowed," *New York Times*, April 9, 2009, http://www.nytimes.com/2009/04/10/business/10norris.html.
38 David Dreman, *Contrarian Investment Strategies: The Psychological Edge* (New York: Simon and Schuster, 1998).
39 Dyan Machan, "The World's Greatest Investors," *SmartMoney*, August 2006, 66.
40 David E. Rye, *25 Stupid Mistakes You Don't Want to Make in the Stock Market* (New York: Contemporary Books, 2002), 230.

41 Allen Roth, "A New Exciting Investing Platform—Kapitall," *Money Watch* (blog), CNBC.com, November 12, 2009, http://www.cbsnews.com/8301-505123_162-37740751/a-new-exciting-investing-platform---kapitall/.

42 Liz Claman, *The Best Investment Advice I Ever Received: Priceless Wisdom from Warren Buffett, Jim Cramer, Suze Orman, Steve Forbes, and Dozens of Other Top Financial Experts* (New York: Warner Business Books, 2006), 185.

43 Alex Tarquinio, "2011 Broker Rankings," *SmartMoney*, June 2011, 56.

44 Neil Parmar and Roy Wolverson, "Brokers 2009," *SmartMoney*, June, 2009, 54–55.

45 "FINRA BrokerCheck®," FINRA, accessed July 20, 2012, http://www.finra.org/Investors/ToolsCalculators/BrokerCheck/.

46 Neil Parmar and Roy Wolverson, "Brokers 2009," *SmartMoney*, June, 2009, 53.

47 Ibid.

48 John R. Nofsinger, *Investment Blunders of the Rich and Famous ... and What You Can Learn from Them* (Upper Saddle River, NJ: Financial Times Prentice Hall, 2002), 213.

49 Lynn O'Shaughnessy, *The Unofficial Guide to Investing* (New York: Macmillan, 1999), 176.

50 Steve Forbes, "Fact and Comment: James W. Michaels," *Forbes*, October 29, 2007, 25.

51 Craig Tolliver, "Net Fund Manager Admits Mistakes," accessed June 22, 2013, *Market Watch, The Wall Street Journal*, October 16, 2000, http://www.marketwatch.com/story/Jacob-admits-mistakes.

52 Richard A. Ferri, "Actively Managed Mutual Funds Are Obsolete," The Bogleheads' View, *Forbes.com*, March 26, 2010, http://www.forbes.com/2010/03/26/index-funds-etfs-actively-managed-obsolete-personal-finance-bogleheads-view-ferri.html.

53 Warren Buffett quoted in *Omaha World Herald*, February 1, 1994.

54 Bill Gross interviewed on "Squawk Box," CNBC, October 19, 2010, http://www.youtube.com/watch?v=cuwHYwyKnZI.

55 Ashby Jones, "Koz Not Done Fighting; Files Cert Petition to the U.S. Supreme Court," *Law Blog, Wall Street Journal*, April 14, 2009.

56 *Benjamin Graham on Investing: Enduring Lessons from the Father of Value Investing*, edited by Rodney G. Klein, updates and commentary by David M. Darst (New York: McGraw Hill, 2009), 105.

57 Reshma Kapadia, "The Survivors," *SmartMoney*, May 2009, 77.
58 Ibid., 80.
59 Ibid., 81.
60 Ibid., 77.
61 Vahan Janjigian, *Even Buffett Isn't Perfect: What You Can—and Can't—Learn from the World's Greatest Investor* (New York: Portfolio, 2009).
62 *Thoughts of Chairman Buffett: Thirty Years of Unconventional Wisdom from the Sage of Omaha*, compiled by Simon Reynolds (New York: HarperCollins, 1998).
63 Dyan Machan, "The World's Greatest Investors," *SmartMoney*, August 2006, 69.
64 Charles R. Morris, *The Sages: Warren Buffett, George Soros, Paul Volcker, and the Maelstrom of Markets* (New York: Perseus Books Group, 2009), 3.
65 Dyan Machan, "The World's Greatest Investors," *SmartMoney*, August 2006, 66.
66 David E. Rye, *25 Stupid Mistakes You Don't Want to Make in the Stock Market* (New York: Contemporary Books, 2002), 267.
67 Ibid.
68 Ibid.
69 Meir Statman interviewed by Charles Wallace, "The 10 Mistakes Investors Most Commonly Make," *Daily Finance*, December 5, 2010.
70 Warren Buffett interviewed on CNBC, March 20, 2009.
71 "Value Investing," *Investopedia*, accessed June 3, 2011, http://www.investopedia.com/terms/v/valueinvesting.asp#axzz2LwI9r9Ww.
72 Gary Belsky and Thomas Gilovich, *Why Smart People Make Big Money Mistakes and How to Correct Them: Lessons from the Life-Changing Science of Behavioral Economics* (New York: Simon and Schuster, 2010).
73 David E. Rye, *25 Stupid Mistakes You Don't Want to Make in the Stock Market* (New York: Contemporary Books, 2002), 157.
74 Neil Parmar and Roy Wolverson, "Brokers 2009," *SmartMoney*, June, 2009, 52.
75 Meir Statman, *What Investors Really Want: Know What Drives Investor Behavior and Make Smarter Financial Decisions* (New York: McGraw Hill, 2010).
76 Roger Lowenstein, *When Genius Failed: The Rise and Fall of Long-Term Capital Management* (New York: Random House, 2001).
77 Liz Claman, *The Best Investment Advice I Ever Received: Priceless Wisdom from Warren Buffett, Jim Cramer, Suze Orman, Steve Forbes,*

and Dozens of Other Top Financial Experts (New York: Warner Business Book, 2006), 75.

78 Tom Taulli, *The Edgar Online Guide to Decoding Financial Statements: Tips, Tools, and Techniques for Becoming a Savvy Investor* (Boca Raton, FL: J. Ross Publishing Inc., 2004).

79 "ProShares Hedge Replication ETF (HDG)," Yahoo! Finance, http://finance.yahoo.com/q?s=hdg&ql=1.

80 Dave Kansas, "How to Read a Stock Chart," in *The Street.com Guide to Smart Investing in the Internet Era: Everything You Need to Know to Outsmart Wall Street and Select Winning Stocks*, (New York: Currency/Doubleday, 2001), 155.

81 Ibid., 156.

82 William P. Barrett "*Safe Places for Cash*," March 12, 2009, assessed August 23, 2013, http://www.forbes.com/forbes/2009/0330/060-cash-is-king.html

83 Esme Faerber, *All About Investing: The Easy Way to Get Started* (New York: McGraw Hill, 2006), 2.

84 Stephanie AuWerter, "Last Minute Retirement Planning," *SmartMoney*, July 9, 2010, accessed August 6, 2011, http://www.smartmoney.com/retirement/planning/last-minute-retirement-planning-16718/.

85 "Retirement Planner," *SmartMoney*, http://www.smartmoney.com/retirement/planner/.

86 William E. Simon quoted in *US News and World Report*, 1979.

87 The Guardian, *GrrlScientist*, http://www.theguardian.com/science/grrlscientist/2012/dec/10/1.

88 "Inflation: Time-Lag to Gold Price Is 14 Months," *The Prudent Investor*, November 29, 2005, http://www.prudentinvestor.com/2005/11/inflation-time-lag-to-gold-price-is-14.html.

89 "Barrick Gold Corporation (ABX)," assessed April 20, 2013, http://finance.yahoo.com/q?s=abx&ql=1.

90 "Newmont Mining Corporation (NEM)," accessed April 20, 2013, http://finance.yahoo.com/q?s=nem&ql=1.

91 "AngloGold Ashanti (AU)," accessed April 20, 2013, http://finance.yahoo.com/q?s=au&ql=1.

92 "DRDGOLD Ltd. (DRD)," accessed June 19, 2013, http://finance.yahoo.com/q?s=drd&ql=1.

93 "Goldcorp, Inc. (GG)," accessed June 19, 2013, http://finance.yahoo.com/q?s=gg&ql=1.

94 "Central Fund of Canada Limited (CEF)," Yahoo! Finance, accessed August 8, 2011, http://finance.yahoo.com/q?s=cef&ql=1.
95 "Central Gold Trust Common GTU," Morningstar, accessed April 28, 2013, http://cef.morningstar.com/quote?t=GTU.
96 "iShares Gold Trust (IAU)," Yahoo! Finance, accessed August 8, 2012, http://finance.yahoo.com/q/pr?s=IAU+Profile.
97 "iShares Gold Trust (IAU)," Yahoo! Finance, accessed August 18, 2012, http://finance.yahoo.com/q/pr?s=IAU+Profile.
98 Thomas E. Woods, Jr., "The Great Gold Robbery of 1933," *Mises Daily*, http://www.mises.org/daily/3056.
99 "iShares Gold Trust (IAU)," Yahoo! Finance, accessed August 18, 2012, http://finance.yahoo.com/q/pr?s=IAU+Profile.
100 "Tiffany & Co. (TIF)," Yahoo! Finance, http://finance.yahoo.com/q?s=tif&ql=1.
101 "Blue Nile Inc. (NILE)," Yahoo! Finance, accessed April 17, 2013, http://finance.yahoo.com/q?s=nile&ql=1.
102 "Signet Jewelers Limited (SIG)," Yahoo! Finance, accessed April 17, 2013, http://finance.yahoo.com/q?s=sig&ql=1.
103 "Zale Corporation (ZLC)," Yahoo! Finance, accessed April 17, 2013, http://finance.yahoo.com/q?s=zlc&ql=1.
104 Meir Statman, *What Investors Really Want: Know What Drives Investor Behavior and Make Smarter Financial Decisions* (New York: McGraw Hill, 2010).
105 "General Motors," *Wikipedia*, accessed September 10, 2012, http://en.wikipedia.org/wiki/General_Motors.
106 "Bondholder Furious over GM Bankruptcy," interview by John Roberts, *American Morning*, CNN, June 1, 2009, http://am.blogs.cnn.com/2009/06/01/bondholder-furious-over-gm-bankruptcy/.
107 Brian Trumbore, "The Collapse of Penn Central," Buy and Hold, accessed July 19, 2012, http://www.buyandhold.com/bh/en/education/history/2001/the_collapse_of_penn_central.htm.
108 Steve Forbes, "Fact and Comment," *Forbes*, October 29, 2007, 25.
109 John Greenwald, "The Wreck of Morrison Knudsen," *Time*, April 3, 1995.
110 Warren Buffett, "You Pay a Very High Price in the Stock Market for a Cheery Consensus," *Forbes*, August 6, 1979, http://www.forbes.com/2008/11/08/buffett-forbes-article-markets-cx_pm-1107stocks.html.

111 Warren Buffett quoted in "Value Investing: Managing the Risks in Value Investing," *Investopedia*, accessed June 11, 2013, http://www.investopedia.com/university/value-investing/value-investing6.asp.
112 "Russell 2000® Index," Russell Investments, http://www.russell.com/indexes/data/fact_sheets/us/russell_2000_index.asp.
113 "Russell 3000® Index," Russell Investments, http://www.russell.com/indexes/data/fact_sheets/us/russell_3000_index.asp.
114 "Wilshire 4500 Completion Index," Wilshire, accessed March 26, 2011, http://web.wilshire.com/Indexes/Broad/Wilshire4500/.

Index

12b-1 fees, 45, 47, 48
1929 market crash, 6–9, 10, 12–13, 14–15, 53
1987 market crash, 19
2001 tech debacle, 6–7, 9, 10, 42, 66
2007 recession, 2, 7, 9, 10, 13, 14, 15, 22, 28, 54

A

A shares, 48
active managed mutual funds, 44
advisor fee, 48
advisors, financial, 35–38, 49
affinity of groups, 31
aggressive growth mutual funds, 43
Ambani, Anil, 22
American Telephone and Telegraph, 54
anger, 29, 34

AngloGold Ashanti, 79
annuities, 37
Apple, Inc., 23, 56, 102
Arnold, Susan, 4
asset-allocation funds, 44
auction rate securities (ARS), 38–39, 49
AutoZone, 23

B

balanced mutual funds, 44
bankruptcy, 85–89, 93
banks, 19, 101–102
Barnes, Brenda, 4
Barrick Gold Corporation, 78
baseline charts, 70
bear market, 94, 96–97, 104
Bear Stearns, 2, 39
Berger, William, 56
Berkshire Hathaway, 52, 55

Bernanke, Ben, 2, 14
best-of-breed stocks, 9, 10, 25, 34, 57, 59, 106
Black Monday, 19, 60
Blixseth, Edra, 21–22
Blixseth, Timothy, 21
Blue Nile Inc., 82
Boeing, 17
bond mutual funds, 44
Boston Marathon bombing, 60
Braly, Angela, 4
breakouts, 65, 71
Bretton Woods system, 17, 25
brokers, 35–38, 49, 98
Buffett, Warren
    2009 losses, 22
    on anger, 29
    on company employees, 51
    on emotions, 27
    first stock purchase, xiv
    on mistakes, 59
    PIMCO and, 52
    tech stocks and, 66
    on uncertainty, 91
    and value investing, 53, 55, 57, 94
bull market, 96–97, 104
Bush, George H. W., 19
Bush, George W., 20, 62
Butner, Brenda, 61
Buttonwood Agreement, 2
buyback, 102

C

call options, 102
Carter, Jimmy, 18
cash, 73–75, 95
cash reserve, 48
Caterpillar, 23
Catz, Safra, 4
central banks, 101–102
Central Fund of Canada, Ltd., 79
Central Gold Trust Common, 79
certificates of deposit (CDs), 75
Chang, Jin Sook, 4
Chapter 11 reorganization, 86
character, 52
Charles Schwab, 64
chart reading, 70
Chevron Corporation, 23
China, 77, 83
Ching, Ho, 3
Citicorp, 9
Citigroup, 55
Citron, Robert, 39
Cliffs Natural Resources, Inc., 23
Clinton, Bill, 19
Clinton, Hillary, 4
closed-end mutual funds, 47
cockroach theory, 56–57
collateral damage, 93, 102
Columbia Business School, 53
commissions, 96, 98
common stock, 106, 107
company financials, 51, 52, 92, 97
company loyalty, 93, 98
company reorganization. *See* corporate restructuring
compounding, 74, 75
consumer price index (CPI), 103
contrarian investors, 63, 104
convertible preferred stock, 106
corporate restructuring, 61, 85, 102
Cramer, Jim, 2, 7, 61

Index

cyclical stocks, 93, 96, 106

D

day trading, 23–24, 34, 49, 51, 59, 61, 64–71, 95, 96, 97
de Dreuzy, Gaspard, 33
deflation, 12, 13
depressions, 14–15, 98
   See also Great Depression
Ding, William, 22–23
Direxion ETFs, 69–70
diversification, 91
dividends, 61
dollar-cost averaging, xv, 7, 40–41, 43, 48, 91, 95, 103
domino effect, 21–24, 25
Dow Jones Composite Average, 107
Dow Jones Industrial Average, 107
DRDGOLD Limited, 79
Dreman, David, 31, 32, 56, 57
durable goods reports, 103
dust storms, 14–15, 95

E

economic news, 61–63, 71
economy
   deflation, 12, 13
   depressions, 14–15, 98
   domino effect and, 21–24, 25
   government reports about, 103–104
   inflation, 12, 13, 73, 74, 77, 103
   shopping and, 20, 62
   stagflation, 12, 13–14, 17, 18
   stock market and, 12, 24
   See also recessions
Edward Jones, 36
Eisenhower, Dwight D., 8, 17
Electronic Exchange (ECN), 108
emerging-market growth mutual funds, 43
emotions, 27–31, 98
employment, 13
   See also unemployment
Enron, 98
equity index fund, 45
eToys, 68
E*Trade, 64
European Central Bank (ECB), 101
exchange-traded funds (ETFs), 44, 45, 68–70
exchange-traded gold funds, 80–81
excitement, 29
expense ratio, 48

F

Faust, Drew, 4
fear, 28–29
Federal Deposit Insurance Corporation (FDIC), 75
federal funds rate, 106
Federal Reserve Bank (the Fed), 2, 7, 14, 18, 19, 55, 81, 101, 106
Fidelity, 63, 64
financial advisors, 35–38, 49
Financial Industry Regulatory Authority (FINRA), 37, 38
financial news, 61–63, 71
financial planners, 74, 75
Finlay Enterprises, 82
flashy presentations, 52, 57

Forbes, Steve, 87
Ford, Gerald, 18
Ford, Henry, 9
Framehawk, 21
fraud, 37–38, 52, 54
full-service firms, 61, 98
fund yield, 48

G

Gallatin, Ronald, 38
Gates, Bill, 21
General Motors, 9, 25, 86
Ginsburg, Ruth Bader, 4
Glickenhaus, Seth, 19, 53, 54–55
global growth mutual funds, 43
gold
    China and, 77, 83
    commodity funds, 79
    exchange-traded gold funds, 80–81
    India and, 78, 82
    inflation and, 77
    jewelry, 82
    Krugerrand coins, 81
    mutual funds, 42, 79
    producers of, 78–79
    rise and fall of, 80
Gold Bullion Security Funds, 79
Goldcorp, Inc., 79
Goldman Sachs, 38
"good till cancelled" order (GTC), 105
Graham, Benjamin, 53, 57
Great Depression, 8, 14–15, 19, 54, 95
greed, 29
Gross, Bill, 52, 53
gross domestic product (GDP), 103
growth mutual funds, 41–43

growth stocks, 107
Gudmundsson, Bjorgolfur, 22

H

Hackett, Jim, 67–68
hard-to-understand products, 38, 49, 92
head-and-shoulders charts, 70
heartfelt feeling, 31, 34
herding, 31, 97

I

income mutual funds, 44
income stocks, 107
incremental purchasing, 91, 97–98
index mutual funds, 44–45
indexes, 107–108
India, 78, 82
inflation, 12, 13, 73, 74, 77, 103
initial public offering (IPO), 105
interest rates, 2, 25, 74, 93, 106
international growth mutual funds, 43
Internet, 63
Internet Kinetics Asset Management Fund, 42
investment advisors, 35–38, 49
investor remorse, 30, 34
investors, types of, 104
iShares Gold Trust (IAU), 80–81
Itel, 52

J

Jacob, Ryan, 42
Jacobs Engineering Group, 23
jargon, 48–49, 101–109

Index

jewelry, gold, 82
J. F. Eckstein and Company, 67
Jones, Paul Tudor, 19
Joy Global, Inc., 23
JPMorgan Chase, 2
June, Debra, 86

K

Kahn, Irving, 53, 55
Kahneman, Daniel, 32
Kansas, Dave, 70
Kapadia, Reshma, 53–55
Kapitall, 33, 34, 99
Kellogg, Peter, 22–23
Kennedy, Joseph, 12, 24
Kernen, Joe, 61
Kozlowski, Dennis, 52
Krugerrand coins, 81

L

Lamont, Thomas W., 7, 8
Lampert, Eddie, 22–23
large-cap growth mutual funds, 42
Lehman Brothers, 38, 39
leverage buying, 98, 104
limit orders, 105
lingo, 48–49, 101–109
load mutual funds, 45–47, 50
London Interbank Offered Rate (LIBOR), 106
long ETFs, 68–70
long-term investors, 55, 57, 59–61, 66, 71, 96, 99, 104
 See also value investors
luck, 12, 24, 53, 57

lump-sum purchases, 65–66, 68, 80, 91, 97
Lynch, Peter, 32

M

Machan, Dyan, 31, 55
Mad Money, 2, 61
Madoff, Bernie, 37–38
management team, 51–53, 57
margin accounts, 65, 71
margin buying, 98, 104
margin calls, 104
market order, 105
markets, 104
market-to-market, 109
market-weighted, 109
Merckle, Adolf, 30
mergers and acquisitions (M&A), 102
Meriwether, John, 67
Merkel, Angela, 3
Merrill Lynch, 36
Michaels, James W., 87
mid-cap growth mutual funds, 43
mistakes, learning from, 32–33, 99
money market mutual funds (MMFs), 44–47
money-market funds, 75
Morningstar rating, 48
Morrison Knudsen, 87–88
mortgages, 2
Mulcahy, Anne, 3
Munger, Charlie, 52
mutual funds
 12b-1 fees, 45, 47, 48
 about, 40–41
 balanced mutual funds, 44

bond mutual funds, 44
dollar-cost averaging and, 40–41, 43, 48
gold, 42, 79
growth mutual funds, 41–43
income mutual funds, 44
jargon, 48–49
money market mutual funds (MMFs), 44–47
net asset value (NAV), 40, 48
prospectus and, 39, 48, 49
researching, 47, 50
risk and, 39
taxes and, 50

N

NASDAQ, 105, 108
National Bureau of Economic Research (NBER), 103
Neff, John, 55
net asset value (NAV), 40, 48
Netease, 23
new issue market (NIM), 105
New York Stock Exchange (NYSE), 2–3, 9, 105, 108
Newmont Mining Corporation, 78–79
Nixon, Richard, 17–18, 25
no-load mutual funds, 47, 48, 50
Nooyi, Indra, 3

O

Obama, Barack, 14, 20
Oceaneering International, Inc., 23
online trading, 61, 63–64, 98
open market, 105
open-end mutual funds, 47
orders, 105–106
Orman, Suze, 4, 73
O'Shaughnessy, Lynn, 39
Over-the-Counter Exchange (OTC), 105, 108

P

Pacific Mutual, 52
Packer, James, 22
Pearlman, Phil, 31
Pelosi, Nancy, 4
Penn Central, xiv, 87
People's Bank of China (PBC), 102
perception, 7–9, 10, 23–24, 25, 32
Pickens, T. Boone, 31
PIMCO, 52
preferred stock, 107
premarket trading, 60, 71, 97, 98
presentations, flashy, 52, 57
Price, T. Rowe, 39
price/earnings ratio (P/E), 56, 57, 94, 102
price-weighted, 109
primary market, 105
prime rate, 106
Private Investment in Public Entities (PIPE), 68
private investors, 68
producer price index (PPI), 104
profit-taking, 91–92, 105–106
program trading, 105
ProShares ETFs, 69–70
prospectus and, 39, 48, 49
put options, 103

Q

Quantum fund, 55–56
Quayle, Dan, 21
Quick, Becky, 61

R

rates of interest, 2, 25, 74, 93, 106
Raymond James, 36
Reagan, Ronald, 18
real-estate market, 18
recessions
   2007 recession, 2, 7, 9, 10, 13, 14, 15, 22, 28, 54
   defined, 15, 25
   depressions and, 14–15
   following a flourishing economy, 10
   investing after, 98
   past recessions, 16–21
   small-business owners and, 21
   types of, 15–16
red flags, 85–89, 94
regret, 28, 30
Reid, Bill, Jr., 38–39
remorse, 30, 34
reorganization. *See* corporate restructuring
resistance price, 70, 71
restructuring. *See* corporate restructuring
retirement planning, 74–75
return on investment (ROI), 48
revenues, 102
reverse splits, 69, 93, 102
the rich
   domino effect and, 21–24, 25
ripple effect. *See* domino effect
risk rating, 48
risk/reward ratio, 60
Roberts, John, 86
Rockefeller, John D., 9
Roosevelt, Franklin D., 16, 81
Rosenfield, Irene, 3
Rowling, J. K., 4
rumors, 60, 92, 96, 98
Russell 2000 Index, 107–108
Russell 3000 Index, 108
Russo, Patricia, 3

S

S&P 500, 107
sadness, 29–30
Salomon Brothers, 54–55, 67
saving, 73–75
Schloss, Walter, 53, 54
secondary financing, 93
secondary market, 105
SecondMarket, 105
sector stocks, 96, 97
secular stocks, 96, 107
Securities and Exchange Commission (SEC), 48
Securities Investor Protection Corporation (SIPC), 106
short ETFs, 68–70
short-sellers, 104
short-term investors, 104
Siebert, Muriel, 3, 4, 10
Signet Jewelers, 82
Simon, William E., 75
single-asset mutual funds, 41–42
small-cap growth mutual funds, 43
smoke-and-mirrors presentations, 52, 57

Social Security, 74
Soros, George, 55–56
SPDR Gold Trust, 80, 81
speculative stocks, 34, 38–39, 49, 67–68, 98
Squawk Box, 52, 61
stagflation, 12, 13–14, 17, 18
Stamper, Roger, 56
Statman, Meir, 27, 30, 59, 65, 85
Stewart, Martha, 4
stock market
    economic indicators and, 12, 94
    investor reactions, 11, 24
    market challenges, 12–14
    market indicators, 6–7
    perception and, 7–9, 10, 23–24, 25, 32
stock market indexes, 107–108
stocks, 106–107
stop sell-limit order, 105
stop-loss order, 7, 105
The Street.com Guide to Smart Investing (Kansas), 70
support price, 70, 71

T

takeover rumors, 92
Taulli, Tom, 68
TD Ameritrade, 64
tech stocks, 42, 66
    See also 2001 tech debacle
Telex, 67, 68
terminology, 48–49, 101–109
Thoratec, 23
Tiffany, 82
trading exchanges, 108
trading range, 65, 71
traditional balanced mutual funds, 44
Treasury-bill futures, 67
trend following, 71–72, 92
trickle-down effect. *See* domino effect
Trimedyne, 68
Truman, Harry S., 16
trust issues, 35
Tversky, Amos, 32
Tyco International, 52

U

UBS, 36
unemployment, 12, 13, 14, 16–18, 20, 95
The Unofficial Guide to Investing (O'Shaughnessy), 39
URS Group, 88
US Treasury-bill futures, 67

V

value investors, 53–56, 57, 66, 104, 106
    See also long-term investors
value mutual funds, 43
values, 109
Vanderheiden, George, 56–57
Vanguard Windsor Value fund, 55
Viacom, 67–68
volatile stocks, 71, 72, 95, 96
Volcker, Paul, 18

W

Wall Street cockroach, 56–57
Walton, Sam, 52
Washington, Dennis, 88

Washington Group International, 88
the wealthy
    domino effect and, 21–24, 25
White Knights, 8
White Motor, 87
White Sewing Machine, 95
Whitman, Margaret, 4
Whitney, Meredith, 61
Whole Foods Market, 23
Wiggin, Albert H., 9
Wilshire 4500, 108
Wilshire 5000, 108
Winfrey, Oprah, 4–5
Woertz, Patricia, 3
women
    college degrees and, 3, 10
    investing and, 10
    and living frugally, 74
    online trading and, 63
    successful examples of, 3–5
Wong, Doris, 82
Wu, Yajun, 4

Y

year-to-date (YTD), 49
Yellowstone Club, 21–22

Z

Zale Corporation, 82

www.ingramcontent.com/pod-product-compliance
Lightning Source LLC
Chambersburg PA
CBHW030758180526
45163CB00003B/1077